Joseph
THE PRIME MINISTER

Joseph
THE PRIME MINISTER

BY THE

Rev. Willam M. Taylor

AmbassadoR

BELFAST ◆ **GREENVILLE**
NORTHERN IRELAND ▼ SOUTH CAROLINA

First Published 1886
This edition 1997

ISBN 1 898787 24 7

AMBASSADOR PRODUCTIONS LTD,
Providence House
16 Hillview Avenue,
Belfast, BT5 6JR
Northern Ireland

Emerald House,
1 Chick Springs Road, Suite 206
Greenville,
South Carolina 29609
United States of America

PREFACE

The general acceptance with which my former volumes of this class have met, and the numerous testimonies to their usefulness with which I have been favoured, have induced me to add another to the series.

The story of Joseph is one of the first favourites of our childhood; and if, in the following pages, I have succeeded in turning it to useful account for the inspiration of the young, the support of those who are bearing the burden and heat of the meridian of life, or the solace of the aged, I shall be deeply grateful.

Wm. M. Taylor
5 West Thirty-fifth Street,
New York

CONTENTS

I   *HIS FATHER'S FAVOURITE* 9

II   *SOLD TO THE ISHMAELITES* 22

III   *CARRIED AWAY INTO SLAVERY* 35

IV   *TEMPTED BUT TRIUMPHANT* 50

V   *THE TWO PRISONERS* 64

VI   *PROMOTION AT LAST* 79

VII   *PUBLIC ADMINISTRATION* 94

VIII   *'CORN IN EGYPT'* 111

IX   *SECOND JOURNEY OF HIS BROTHERS TO EGYPT* 125

X   *JACOB AND HIS SONS REMOVE TO EGYPT* 140

X   *I JOSEPH'S TWO VISITS TO HIS AGED FATHER* 156

XII   *JACOB'S DYING PROPHECIES* 174

XIII   *JACOB'S FUNERAL* 193

XIV   *JOSEPH'S DEATH* 209

XV   *THE CHARACTER AND CAREER OF JOSEPH* 226

JOSEPH

THE

PRIME-MINISTER.

I.

HIS FATHER'S FAVOURITE.

Genesis xxxvii. 1-11.

THE influence of Jacob's experience at Peniel was not limited to the brief time of its actual existence. That night was the water-shed of his life, marking the "henceforth" from which he became another man. Till then he had been, in nature as well as in name, Jacob the Supplanter. While yet in his father's house he had taken a mean advantage of Esau's necessity to get possession of the birthright; and notwithstanding the Bethel vision, the same disposition had re-appeared in his dealings with Laban. He had, indeed, many good things about him, notably a rapid intelligence, great capacity for work, ready resourcefulness, and steady perseverance; yet these were greatly vitiated by the cunning and unscrupulous selfishness to which they were all made to minister. He was markedly deficient in those qualities which give attractiveness to character, and we cannot see that he was animated by any great religious principle for at least the larger portion of his residence at Padan-aram.

But the new name given to him by the angel at Peniel
was given to a new man, and for the remaining fifty years
of his life the Supplanter in him disappears and the
Prince of God comes into view.   Henceforth he is guile-
less as Nathaniel.   Deceit in him gives place to truth, and
duplicity to singleness of mind.   As one has very well
expressed it, " Spiritually he halts when before he would
have put down his foot unfaltering.   He hears of the
indignity done to Dinah, and ' holds his peace.'   Simeon
and Levi avenge the wrong by a deed of shameless deceit
and cruelty, and he says to them, ' Ye have troubled me
to make me to stink among the inhabitants of the land.'
A still more shameless deed than the one done at Shechem
is committed in his own household, and all that is said of
him is that ' he heard it.'   Trial follows trial, bereavement succeeds bereavement ; under severe and protracted
discipline the higher spiritual nature grows and ripens till
at the close the piety of Abraham and Isaac—their faith
in God and in His special promises—shines forth in Jacob
in unclouded beauty." *

From   Peniel, after   his   reconciliation   to   Esau and
peaceful parting from him, Jacob went to Succoth, and
thence to Shechem, where Abraham reared his first altar
in the Land of Promise.   Here, as it would seem, he meant
to take up his permanent abode, for he bought a piece of
ground and dug in it that well which is now imperishably
associated with one of the sweetest incidents in the life
of our Saviour, and which remains till this day an object
of deepest interest to every traveller in the Holy Land.
But the treacherous treatment of the sons of Shechem by
Simeon and Levi in the matter of Dinah drove him from
that beautiful valley, and under the direction of God he
went first to Bethel, where Rachel died in giving birth

* Dr. William Hanna in " The Patriarchs," p. 16.

to Benjamin, and afterwards to Hebron, where his father
Isaac was still living.

It is at this point we take up the story in the chapter
now before us, and begin the life of Joseph; and it may
surprise some of you that I should speak of Isaac as
surviving till this date, inasmuch as the account of his
death and burial is given at the close of the thirty-fifth
chapter, and so precedes the narrative on which we are now
entering. But in reality the death of Isaac did not take
place until twelve years after Joseph was sold into slavery,
and the account of it is inserted where we find it in order
to give completeness to that section or sub-division of
the history which treats especially of Isaac.

If you examine the book of Genesis with care you will
discover that it consists of eleven sections, nine of which
begin with the phrase " These are the generations of,"
and one with the words " This is the book of the generations of." These may have been—indeed, probably were
—ancient documents, existing long before the book itself
was put together by Moses; but he, under Divine guidance,
used them and endorsed them, so that we may rely on
their veracity. Now the book about Isaac begins with
the nineteenth verse of the twenty-fifth chapter, and ends
with the twenty-ninth verse of the thirty-fifth chapter.
Naturally, therefore, it includes the account of his death
and burial, and concludes with it. It is followed, in the
thirty-sixth chapter, with the generations of Ishmael, and
in the thirty-seventh with those of Jacob, who, now that
he has returned to Canaan and has become a son of
Abraham, not according to the flesh merely, but in faith
and character, is for the first time recognised in this
formal way as the head of the covenant people. But in
giving the needful details about Jacob, the chronicler goes
back to things which occurred before the death of Isaac,
and, therefore, to avoid confusion, as well as to get a clear

idea of the circumstances of Joseph's boyhood, it may be well for us to go a little into detail.

According, then, to the commonly received chronology, Jacob was ninety-seven years old when he returned from Padan-aram, and Isaac was 157. At the same date Joseph was a boy of six. When our story opens he was a lad of seventeen. Isaac was 168, and Jacob 108. Now, when Isaac died his days were an hundred and fourscore years, so that he must have lived at Hebron twelve years after Joseph was sold into slavery by his brethren. If, then, we allow six years for the sojourn of Jacob at Shechem and Bethel before he came to Hebron, we will get the result, conjectural, indeed, but still probable, that Joseph lost his mother Rachel before he was twelve years old, and that he lived for at least five years in Hebron in the neighbourhood of his grandfather Isaac.

These facts will help us to reproduce in our imagination the early years of that wonderful boy whose history has charmed every reader—the oldest as well as the youngest —by its simple naturalness, its undying interest, and its "penetrating pathos." At the head of one encampment was the venerable Isaac, quiet, retiring, unobtrusive in his disposition as of yore, withal frail with age and enfeebled by disease, and so not able to take much active part in the arrangement of affairs; but all the more at leisure, because of that, to give some affectionate attention to the mother-less boy, in whom he recognised the heir of the birthright which Reuben had forfeited, and to whom, therefore, he would be drawn by a peculiar attraction. Who can tell how much Joseph received of religious instruction and of never-to-be-forgotten truth from the lips of his meditative grandsire? Is it a mere fancy which supposes that in these early years Joseph learned from Isaac the wonderful story of Moriah, and so had begotten in him that faith in the covenant of his God, and in the nearness of Jehovah to him in every time of trial and temptation, by which he was sustained in later life? I am no painter, but if I were I should like to try my hand at the portrayal of the young Joseph sitting at the feet of the blind old Isaac, and listening with wonder to the recital of his experience on that eventful day when he was rescued from sacrifice by the angel's interference, and had his first insight into the world beyond.

At the head of the other encampment was Jacob, with the Peniel glow still upon his character, if not also on his face, and his heart chastened and saddened by the death of his beloved Rachel, yet finding a sweet solace in the baby Benjamin, whom she had left behind, and even more in her eldest son, to whom the birthright now legitimately belonged. That fact gave him at first, as I suppose, importance in his father's eyes, and out of that and the winsomeness and intelligence of the boy himself grew the partiality which he so unwisely manifested for him.

But in the one encampment of Jacob there were four divisions, forming not separate households, indeed, but yet far more dangerous, so far as the preservation of harmony was concerned, than if they had been entirely distinct. These were composed of Leah and her sons, Zilpah and her sons, Bilhah and her sons, and the sons of Rachel; and from what we learn elsewhere of Joseph's ten half-brothers, we may be sure that they had little scruple in riding roughshod over the feelings and wishes of any one who seemed in the least degree to stand in their way. This disposition of his brethren, added to his own motherless condition, would send Joseph much in upon himself, and make him, from his precocity in his experience of adversity, a welcome companion to his father. And little harm might have come of that if Jacob had not been unwise in the manifestation of his preference. One would have thought that the recollection of his own experience might have prevented him from falling into such a mistake. He might have asked himself how he had liked the favouritism of his father for Esau, or what good had come out of Rebekah's preference for himself above Esau. But, untaught by the consequences of the folly of his own parents, he repeats the same himself; for he set Joseph over the sons of Bilhah and the sons of Zilpah, giving him the charge of them in their daily labour, whether as shepherds or as agriculturists. No doubt Joseph was particularly wise for his years ; for that, according to some, is the meaning of the phrase, "a son of the old ones," here translated "a son of old age"; but still, to put the younger over the older was pre-eminently foolish, and could tend only to provoke enmity in those who were thus humiliated.

This feeling would be intensified by his giving to Joseph a peculiar dress which was intended to mark his superiority. In our version it is called "a coat of many colours," as if its peculiarity consisted in its variegated appearance. But modern scholars are of opinion that the words describe "a tunic reaching to the extremities," or, as in the margin of the Revised Version, "a long garment with sleeves," and so refer to the shape rather than to the fabric ; though from the fact that on one of the Egyptian tombs at Beni Hassan there is a representation of a train of captives who are clad in party-coloured garments, it is not impossible that the tunic here specified was ornamented with many-coloured stripes. In any case, it was meant as a badge of distinction and superiority for Joseph as the heir of the birthright and the favourite of his father, and so the very sight of it embittered the hearts of his brethren against him.

The evil was aggravated, also, by the conduct of Joseph himself, "for he brought unto his father their evil report." This has generally been understood as implying that Joseph

was a petty tale-bearer, and carried to his father accounts
of the doings of his brethren, which were designed by him
to get them into trouble. But I cannot quite accept that
view of the case. My reading of the history is that
Jacob set Joseph over the sons of the handmaids, and that
the report which he carried was that which was required
of him in his capacity of overseer. It was a most unwise
thing in Jacob to put Joseph into such a position; but,
being in it, he had to be faithful and give an account of the
manner in which each performed his duties, and that irri-
tated his brethren and stirred them up to intense hatred of
him.

Then matters were made still worse by his dreams. He
told them with the utmost simplicity, but they carried their
interpretation on their face, and the repetition of the same
forecast, under different symbolism, intensified the provo-
cation. His brethren were in no mood to do obeisance to
him, and even his father, though he resolved to keep watch
and see if God had really been revealing the future to his
son, blamed him for what seemed to be his pride.

It is not said in the record that his dreams were prophetic, and some have preferred to believe that they came
like any ordinary visions, taking their shape from the
general current of Joseph's thoughts when he was awake.
If that be the correct view of the case, then Joseph must
have been of a most ambitious nature, and the knowledge
that he was now the heir of the birthright must have so
filled his imagination as to give definiteness and coherence
even to his dreams. That is not an impossibility—and if
any one chooses to accept such an account of the matter,
I see nothing either rationalistic or unbelieving in his doing
so. But still, that view scarcely seems to me to be in
harmony with the beautiful humility which comes out in
Joseph's character, and appears to be inconsistent with the
simple *naïveté* manifested by him in telling his dreams to

his brethren. The ambitious man is invariably a silent man. He keeps his own forecasts to himself. He does not make common talk of his schemes and his dreams. He will not " show his hand " in the game, lest he should give another the means of defeating that for which he designs to play. Therefore the fact that Joseph told his dreams to his brethren is an indication to me that there was no ambition in his soul. They were not the crystallisation into the symbols of visions of the thoughts which were filling his mind all through his waking hours, but came, as I believe, in the way of Divine revelation, and were among the early links in that chain of providences which ultimately led the family of Jacob to Egypt, where they could better grow into a nation than they could among the Canaanites. But however that may have been, the very telling of them inflamed the hatred of his brethren against him, and moved them to take measures to put him out of the way.

Before we follow them in the carrying out of their malicious intentions, however let us pause here, and glean a few of the lessons which we may learn from this narrative for our daily guidance.

We are taught here the evil of favouritism in the family. The balance, as between the different children in the same household, must be held evenly by the parents. They may have different dispositions, and there may be that in one which is more attractive than anything in another. One may be brighter, or more amiable, or more companionable than another, but before the discipline of the family they ought to be all on a level. They are all alike the children of the father, and should be dealt with by him on principles of the strictest equity. It is true that in some respects their differences of disposition will require differences of treatment, but they should be all kept on an equality. No one ought to be the " pet " of either father or mother, for the " pet " is apt to become petted, haughty, and arrogant towards the others ; while the showing of constant favour to him alienates the affections of the rest, both from him and from the parents. *"Is that you Pet ?"* said a father from his bedroom to a little one who stood at the door in the early morning knocking for admission. *"No, it isn't Pet, it's only me,"* replied a sorrowful little voice ; and that was the last of " pet " in that family. See what mischief it occasioned here in Jacob's household! No doubt there were special dangers in such a case as his, for there were four families in one, and it must have been hard to preserve harmony at all ; but that only made it the more important that every irritating influence should be, as far as possible, removed, and it was the greatest folly in Jacob to make such a display of his preference for Joseph. We see the same thing in even a worse form in the household of Isaac, where each parent had a favourite, and both worked at cross-purposes. Such a system of partiality usually ends in the " spoiling "—to use the common, but expressive, word — of the favourite himself ; and even where, as in Joseph's case, that danger is escaped, it alienates from him the other members of the family, and provokes them to insubordination. Above and beyond most other things, therefore, family government must be just, and the balance must be held by the parent with the most unswerving impartiality.

We may learn also from this narrative how bitter is the antagonism of the wicked to the righteous in the world. The partiality of Jacob for Joseph furnished the occasion for the hatred of his brethren, and is to be unhesitatingly condemned ; but the real root of it was deeper, and is to be traced to the fact that Joseph would not consent to be one of them, and join them in the doing of things which they knew that their father would condemn. He held himself aloof from their wickednesses. His conscience

was tender, his heart was pure, his will was firm. He
was a Puritan, and they were regardless, and they chose
to set down his nonconformity to pride rather than to
principle, and persecuted him accordingly. They supposed
that his refusal to identify himself with them was caused
by his thinking himself superior to them, and they re-
taliated by breaking off all intercourse with him; for
when it is said that "they could not speak peaceably unto
him," or, as the phrase literally is, "they could not say
salaam to him," the meaning virtually is, in modern
parlance, that they "cut" him, and treated him most
disrespectfully and discourteously.

But have we nothing like this in our modern life? It
may not be very common between brothers, though, alas!
it is not quite unknown even between them; but go into
our schools, our colleges, our stores, or our workshops,
and you may frequently find that the most unpopular
scholars, or students, or clerks, or artisans are those who
hold themselves aloof from the excesses, the follies, or the
sins of the rest. Their presence is a constant protest
against the doings of the others; their conduct is a con-
tinuous condemnation of that of the others, and they are
hated simply because of that. The Athenians became tired
of hearing Aristides called "the just," and they banished
him to get rid of that which was disagreeable; so those
who are unprincipled become intolerant of the integrity of
the upright who are working at their side, and do everything in their power to make them uncomfortable. There
is an immense amount of petty persecution of this sort
going on in all our colleges, commercial establishments,
and factories, of which the principals and the great world
seldom hear, but which shows us that the human nature
of to-day is in its great features identical with that which
existed many centuries ago in the family of Jacob. What
then? Are the upright to yield? are they to abate their

protest? are they to become even as the others? No; for that would be to take the leaven out of the mass; that would be to let evil become triumphant, and so that must never be thought of. Let the persecuted in these ways hold out. Let them neither retaliate, nor recriminate, nor carry evil reports, but let them simply hold on, believing that "he that endureth overcometh." Having done all things, let them "*stand*," and in the end those who now decry them will be compelled to do them honour. Yes, these two dreams of Joseph are here for just such as those whom I have been now describing, and they tell them, as they told him, that by-and-bye—it may be after long suffering and much privation, but yet ultimately—the sheaves of their persecutors will make obeisance to their sheaves, and those who now "send them to Coventry" will yet be glad to do homage at their feet.

But now the case of Joseph here brings up the whole question of our responsibility in regard to what we see or hear that is evil in other people, and it may be well to say a few words concerning that. I have come to the conclusion that Joseph was by his father placed in formal charge of his brothers, and that it was his duty to give a truthful report concerning them, even as to-day an overseer is bound in justice to his employer to state precisely the kind of service which those under him are rendering. That is no tale-bearing; that is simple duty. But now, suppose we are invested with no such charge over another, and yet we see him do something that is deplorably wrong, what is our duty in such a case? Are we bound to carry the report to his father or to his employer, or must we leave things alone and let them take their course? The question *so* put is a delicate one and very difficult to handle. But I think I see two or three things that cast some little light upon it.

We are not bound by any law, human or divine, to act

the part of a detective on our neighbour and lay ourselves out for the discovery of that in him which is disreputable or dishonest.   We must have detectives in the department of police, and they are very serviceable there ; but that every one of us should be closely watching every other to see what evil he can discover in him is intolerable, and we should discourage in all young people every tendency to such peering Paul-pryism.

When, without any such deliberate inspection on our part, we happen to see that which is wrong, we should, in the way in which we treat the case, make a distinction between a crime and a vice.   A crime is that which is a violation of the civil law ; a vice is that which, without violating the civil law, is a sin against God.   Now suppose that what we see is a crime—the young man, let us say, is robbing his employer—then my clear duty, if I would not be a *particeps criminis*, is to give information to his master, and let him deal with the case as he sees fit.   On the other hand, if the evil is a vice—which does not, directly at least, interfere with his efficiency as a servant—then I must deal with himself alone.   My duty in such a case is to hold my peace to others, and to speak faithfully to the young man himself.   If he hear me, then I have gained him ; but if he refuse to hear me, then I may say to him that, as he has chosen to pay no heed to my expostulation, I shall feel it my duty to inform his father of the matter ; and then, having acted out that determination, I may consider that my responsibility in regard to him is at an end, unless, in God's providence, there is given me some other opening through which to approach him.

These principles seem to me to be very plain and very practicable ; but I can go no further in the matter, and must say that, for the rest, each should do as occasion serves.   We cannot do wrong, however, to follow the wise advice of Lawson, as thus given in connection with the passage on which we have been commenting : " When we see any man's children disgracing and hurting themselves, if we cannot by our own influence persuade them to refrain, we will deserve the thanks of their parents by letting them know how much they are dishonoured, and what grief is likely to be brought upon them by their children if they are not checked. If parents are to admonish or to correct their children for bad behaviour, it is necessary for them to inspect their conduct ; but they cannot be always under their own eyes, and therefore they ought to reckon themselves indebted to the persons who assist them, by prudent and seasonable information, in this part of their duty. Yet great caution must be used in this office of love, that we may not bring upon ourselves the guilt and reproach of officious interference in other men's matters." *

The whole thing lies in that phrase, "this office of love." It is to be performed in affection, not to make mischief, but to save a soul ; and if we keep that motive uppermost we shall not be likely to go far astray. " Brethren, if a man be overtaken in a fault, ye who are spiritual restore such an one in the spirit of meekness, considering thyself lest thou also be tempted." Take the gospel principles underlying that command and apply them to the case which we have supposed, then you will reach its true solution.

---

* " Lectures on the History of Joseph," by George Lawson, D.D., p. 3.

II.

SOLD TO THE ISHMAELITES.

GENESIS XXXVII. 12-35.

WHEN envy has fully formed its purpose of cruelty, it very speedily sees and seizes an opportunity for carrying it through. The great dramatist, indeed, has represented one of the most unscrupulous of his characters as excusing himself after this fashion : " How oft the sight of means to do ill deeds makes ill deeds done "; but then it is only the envious and malicious man who is on the outlook for means to do ill deeds, and therefore it is to him only that the perception of them offers a temptation. If King John had not been wishing to make away with Arthur, the presence of Hubert would not have suggested to him that he had found a fit instrument to do what he desired. Just as love keens the vision to such a degree that it sees ways of service that are invisible to others, so hate quickens the perception, and finds an occasion for its gratification in things that would have passed unnoticed by others. The brothers of Joseph, therefore, being filled with envy towards him, soon had an opportunity of working their will upon him, and they seized it with an eagerness which showed how intensely they hated him.

They had gone with their flocks to Shechem, where, as we saw in the last chapter, their father had purchased a parcel of ground, in which he had digged a well. This place, now known as the valley of Nâblus, is perhaps

the most fertile as well as the most beautiful in all
Palestine. It was more than two days' journey north
from Hebron, where Jacob now had his abode; and
perhaps the recent fued between the Shechemites and
his sons, in the matter of Dinah, made the patriarch
somewhat anxious as to their welfare. He had already
had bitter experience of the hasty and vindictive disposition of some of the members of his family, and it is
quite likely that he feared lest they should become again
embroiled with the inhabitants of Shechem. Therefore
he sent Joseph, saying, "Go, I pray thee, see whether
it be well with thy brethren, and well with the flocks,
and bring me word again." Such a mission seems to us,
on the first blush of it, at once too important and too
dangerous for so young a man. But Joseph had already
manifested great ability, and secured his father's confidence; and Dr. Thomson tells us that among the
modern Arab tribes it is not unusual for individuals
to go a long way "from their encampments on errands
often perilous."* Perhaps Joseph had been sent forth
on similar commissions more than once before, and so
there would be on this occasion the less misgiving, either
on Jacob's part to bid him go or on Joseph's to set out.
But, in any case, though their parting seemed a common-
place matter, and they expected to be re-united in a few
days at the longest, yet they did not look upon each
other's faces again for more than twenty years. Could
they have foreseen all that was before them in that long
interval, with what different emotions would they have
bidden each other farewell! But for them, as it is still
for us, the future was mercifully concealed, and they had
to go forward into it only one step at a time.

When Joseph arrived at Shechem he discovered that

---

* "The Land and the Book: Central Palestine and Phœnicia," p. 169.

his brethren had gone from their usual pasturage with
their flocks ; and when he was wandering about in search
of them, uncertain what he should do, he was found by an
obliging stranger, who told him that he had heard his
brethren say, " Let us go to Dothan." Therefore he went
some twelve miles farther after them, and came to that place
the name of which signifies " two wells," and the situation
of which is marked by Eusebius as twelve miles to the
north of Samaria. It has been discovered in modern times
by Van de Velde and Dr. Robinson, still bearing its ancient
name, and it is described as located at the south end of a
plain of the richest pasturage, four or five miles south-west
of Jenin, and separated only by a swell or tier of hills
from the plain of Esdraelon. Near it are now large under-
ground cisterns, such as in that country are apt to become
dry, and these are of the same sort as the pit into which,
as we shall by-and-bye see, Joseph was put. Even to this
day it has the best pasturage in all the region, and in that
fact, though the narrative is silent upon the point, we
have probably the reason why the sons of Jacob came to
it at this time ; for, as Hackett suggests, " It is the very
place which herdsmen, such as they were, would naturally
seek, after having exhausted the supplies of their previous
pasture-ground." * But perhaps most interesting of all,
this Dothan is on the present line of travel between the
country to the east of the Jordan and Egypt ; and Mr
Tristram speaks of having met there "a long caravan of
mules and asses, laden, on their way from Damascus to
Egypt," so that the whole story is confirmed by most
minute correspondences between the ancient record and
the modern locality.

In the immediate neighbourhood there is a fountain,
and Thomson suggests that the brothers might have

---

* See Smith's " Dictionary," art. DOTHAN.

watered their flocks thereat, or might have been seated round it on the grass when they caught their first glimpse of Joseph from afar. But the sight only crystallised their envy into purpose, and determined them to wreak their vengeance on him. They were far from home. There was no one to interfere with them or to bear testimony against them. They would never have a better opportunity of putting him out of the way, and no one would be the wiser. Therefore they said one to another—that is, the suggestion sprung up, as it were, simultaneously among them, and was not due to any one more than another, but was the spontaneous ejaculation of all at once—" Behold, this dreamer cometh! Come now, therefore, and let us slay him, and cast him into some pit ; and we will say, ' Some evil beast hath devoured him' ; and we shall see what will become of his dreams!" Still harping on his dreams! But why should they thus stultify themselves? If there was nothing in the dreams, they were utterly beneath their notice ; but if God's revelation was in them, it was beyond their power to frustrate them. Thus in either case it was useless for them to attempt to do anything about them. But their blood was up. Joseph had been put over them, and had humiliated them with their father, and he must be got rid of. So they said, " Let us slay him!" How true the words of the Apostle: " He that hateth his brother is a murderer!" and how natural for an infuriated and selfish man it is to take " the way of Cain," and travel along it to the bitter end!

But in the present instance there was one honest effort made to prevent mischief, and it was made by him from whom it might have been least expected. For Reuben had, as a punishment for his grievous and revolting sin, been deprived of the birthright, and it might have been supposed that he would have been the most implacable of them all towards Joseph, who had been put into his place.

But his was a better nature, with all its faults, than that evinced by Simeon and Levi, and before the history closes we shall have again occasion to remark on the chivalry which he showed. Yet the good in him was spasmodic and intermittent. He was too much a creature of mere impulse, and so he came in at last for the characterisation from his father, " Unstable as water, thou shalt not excel." In the present emergency he showed his prudence by seeming to fall in with the general sentiment of his brethren, while at the same time he sought to keep it from doing mischief. He boarded the train which he could not arrest, but he boarded it with the purpose of ultimately controlling it and so preventing a catastrophe. The motive was good, but I am not quite so sure about the policy. It savours a little too much of worldly wisdom, and little good came out of it in the end. We have seen it tried here often enough in politics, and almost always with this result, that the well-meaning men who have gone into a questionable movement under the idea that they could thereby guide it into something that would be at least harmless have been themselves outwitted and befooled. It would have been just about as easy for Reuben to have stood out against the persecution of Joseph altogether as it was for him to protest against the shedding of his blood, and it might have been equally efficacious. At any rate, it would have exonerated him from the guilt which they all alike ultimately incurred.

His plan was to deliver Joseph, but in a way that was itself deceptive, for he seemed to be doing one thing while he was really seeking another. His proposal was that they should put Joseph into a pit. That to them looked to be a refinement on their cruelty, for it left him to starve to death, while they had meant that he should be slain out of hand. As such, therefore, it commended itself to their acceptance. But his secret intention was to come back by himself when the others should be out of the way, and then take him out and return with him to his father. It was well meant, and not very badly planned either; but then it required that a very careful watch should be maintained, and just there the instability of Reuben's character came in to mar it all; for, thinking that now the crisis was past, he went away, and took no further oversight of the matter, and in his absence it was all upset. For the moment, however, it looked as if he had succeeded, for the others accepted his suggestion, and, after stripping Joseph of his hated coat, they put him into one of those cisterns which were so common in Palestine, and which, when dry, were sometimes, as in the case of Jeremiah, used as a prison. Lieutenant Anderson, of the Palestine Exploration Enterprise, thus writes regarding them : " The numerous rock-hewn cisterns that are found everywhere would furnish a suitable pit in which they might have thrust him; and as these cisterns are shaped like a bottle, with a narrow mouth, it would be impossible for any one imprisoned within it to extricate himself without assistance. These cisterns are now all cracked and useless ; they are, however, the most undoubted evidences that exist of the handiwork of the inhabitants in ancient times." *

But what of Joseph all this time? There is no word in the narrative here to tell us how he felt. Only one glimpse of him do we get, and that is long afterwards, when his brothers were in the Egyptian prison, and they said one to another, " We are verily guilty concerning our brother, in that we saw the anguish of his soul when he besought us and we would not hear."† But what a glimpse that is, and how much it reveals ! First, when

---

* " The Land and the Book : Central Palestine and Phœnicia," p. 168.
† Genesis xlii. 21.

the part of a detective on our neighbour and lay ourselves
out for the discovery of that in him which is disreputable
or dishonest.   We must have detectives in the department
of police, and they are very serviceable there ; but that
every one of us should be closely watching every other to
see what evil he can discover in him is intolerable, and
we should discourage in all young people every tendency
to such peering Paul-pryism.

When, without any such deliberate inspection on our
part, we happen to see that which is wrong, we should,
in the way in which we treat the case, make a distinction
between a crime and a vice.   A crime is that which is
a violation of the civil law ; a vice is that which, without
violating the civil law, is a sin against God.   Now
suppose that what we see is a crime—the young man,
let us say, is robbing his employer—then my clear duty,
if I would not be a *particeps criminis*, is to give information
to his master, and let him deal with the case as he sees
fit.   On the other hand, if the evil is a vice—which does
not, directly at least, interfere with his efficiency as a
servant—then I must deal with himself alone.   My duty
in such a case is to hold my peace to others, and to speak
faithfully to the young man himself.   If he hear me, then
I have gained him ; but if he refuse to hear me, then I
may say to him that, as he has chosen to pay no heed
to my expostulation, I shall feel it my duty to inform his
father of the matter ; and then, having acted out that
determination, I may consider that my responsibility in
regard to him is at an end, unless, in God's providence,
there is given me some other opening through which
to approach him.

These principles seem to me to be very plain and very
practicable ; but I can go no further in the matter, and
must say that, for the rest, each should do as occasion
serves.   We cannot do wrong, however, to follow the

passing by Dothan, made their appearance, and Judah at once conceived the idea of getting a profit out of the business, and ridding themselves of their brother too by selling him into slavery. They immediately agreed to this new proposal, and so for twenty pieces of silver—about three pounds of our money—they sold him to the traders, who are here called Ishmaelites and Midianites, either because these had already become the generic names for merchants or because they were the descendants of those sons of Abraham who, nearly 200 years before, had gone out to make their own way in the world.

The sequel is soon told. Reuben, returning to the pit, was grievously disappointed, and rent his clothes with a grief as violent as it was short-lived. The others, feeling it necessary to give some account of Joseph's disappearance to their father, took the exasperating coat and dipped it in the blood of a kid and brought it to Jacob, and said, " This have we found : know now whether it be thy son's coat or no." The effect was terrible ; the patriarch was overwhelmed with sorrow, for he knew the coat perfectly, and the story seemed to be so well confirmed that he said, " Joseph is without doubt rent in pieces." They tried to comfort him, but it was all in vain, and no wonder, considering who the consolers were. Reuben could have told him all the truth, but that would only have put him into the deeper agony of suspense ; and therefore, perhaps out of kindness, he preferred to let his father rest in the false certainty that Joseph was dead. Or it may be that in putting the matter thus we are doing Reuben too much honour, for it is possible that he feared for his own safety if he should do as Joseph had done and tell his brothers' evil report. But surely this was a case in which it was a clear duty to tell all the truth, no matter whom it shamed.

Now, leaving Joseph for the time in the hands of the slave-merchants, let us lift out of this narrative, with which we have all been familiar from our childhood, some important lessons for the regulation of our manhood. We may be reminded by it of the uncertainties that characterise our human existence. How true it is that we know not what a day may bring forth! Joseph goes out on his father's errand and never more returns to his father's house—does not see his father again, in fact, for twenty-two years. Of course the crime of his brothers was the cause of this long separation between him and his venerable parent. But how often similar things occur even among ourselves! Some years ago a little boy was stolen from his home in Philadelphia, and though every means that affection could suggest or professional skill could devise have been used for his discovery, the mystery has never been cleared up, so that to this hour his parents are in most horrible suspense. In our own city, too, scarcely a week elapses without the announcement that some one has disappeared from home and business, and very frequently nothing more is heard of him.

But, apart from such occurrences, which may be traced to the cunning and malignity of wicked men, and which are a disgrace to our much boasted civilisation, how often it happens, in the simple providence of God, and without blame to any one, that those who part in the morning with the hope of meeting again in a very short while never see each other more on earth! The street accident causes death; or the sudden outbreak of fire in the building in which their office hours are spent cuts off all possibility of escape, and they are burned to ashes; or a panic in a crowded place of amusement which they visited has caused a great loss of life, and they are numbered among the victims; or a railway collision has smashed the train in which they were passengers, and they are reported among the dead; or, without any such catastrophe, they have simply yielded to a sudden paroxysm of illness and passed within the veil. Who knows not how frequently such things are occurring in the midst of us, so that, as we have had occasion again and again to notice, the proverb is verified that it is "the unexpected that happens." What then? Are we to have our hearts forever darkened with the shadow of the possibility of such things coming to us? No; for that would be to make our lives continually miserable; but the lesson is that we should be ever ready to respond to the call of God, and should take short views of things by living, as nearly as possible, a day at a time. We need not borrow trouble on the strength of the uncertainty to which I have referred, for " sufficient unto the day is the evil thereof"; but we ought to be taught by it to finish every day's work in its own day, since its lesson is, " Boast not thyself of to-morrow, for thou knowest not what a day may bring forth."

But we may see from this narrative that the beginning of sin is like the letting out of water. The aperture is small at first, but the force of the current increases the size of the outlet, and that in its turn makes the stream larger and stronger; or, to put it in language without any figure, one sin begets another, so that what began in envy leads to murder, and that again gives birth to falsehood. Sin thus multiplies as rapidly as the Colorado beetle, and no matter what may be the first one, you may always call its name Gad, for you may surely say, " a troop cometh." Therefore, if we would successfully resist it, we must withstand its beginnings. This is true of every sin, but it is more especially so of envy, which, as Taylor Lewis has remarked in connection with this very history, has in it something very peculiar, fully justifying the calling of it diabolical. For it is a purely *soul* sin, not traceable at all to the body, or in any way connected with it; not having in it anything that has any resemblance to good, but being only unmingled evil. It is the hatred of a man for the good that is in him, and so, to use Dr. Lewis's language, "It is the breath of the old serpent. It is pure devil, as it is also purely spiritual. It needs no body, no concupiscent organisation, no appetites or fleshly motions, no nerves even, for the exercise of its devilish energies. It is a soul-poison, yet acting fearfully upon the body itself, bringing more death into it than seemingly stronger and more tumultuous passions that have their nearer seat in the fleshly nature. It is 'rottenness in the bone.'"* Be on your guard, then, against yielding to any one sin, for it will speedily open the door of your heart to many others; and be specially on your guard against the Satanic mother sin of envy.

But mere negative measures here will not suffice. The hatred of a man for the good that is in him must be supplanted by the love of Christ, and then what Chalmers calls "the expulsive power of a new affection" will come into operation. You expel darkness with light, and you shut evil out of the heart by the admission into it of Christ.

We may learn that in seeking to defeat God's purposes we are all the while unconsciously helping on their fulfilment. These brothers of Joseph were bent on making the realisation of his dreams impossible, and yet the thing which they did was one step towards the bringing about of the elevation of their brother. They were ignorant of that at the time, but they were made to see it afterwards; and I specially call your attention to the fact that here they were working under no constraint. Nobody compelled them to give up their first idea of putting Joseph to death. The proposal to put him into a pit was purely spontaneous with Reuben, and they were at liberty to act upon it or not as they chose. The same thing was true of the suggestion of Judah about selling him to the Ishmaelites;

---

* See note in Lange's "Genesis," p. 589.

and yet thus freely working, as they thought, for the falsification of his dreams, they were, after all, only helping to bring them to pass. Here is the whole of God's providence in miniature—the Ishmaelites came past in the very nick of time, just at the moment when Joseph was in the pit; their presence suggested to Judah the idea of selling Joseph to them, and the rest of the brothers fell in with the proposal. Each party was seeking its own ends, and yet they were all contributing to bring about the purpose of God concerning Joseph. We cannot explain the "law" of it, but we clearly see the fact. Oh! the marvellous wisdom of that providence of God which thus, without doing violence to the will of any human being, lays all their actions under tribute for the furtherance of its designs! And what is the use of a man's trying to thwart God's purposes when, whether he will or not, everything he does only helps them forward? Surely it is better far to acquiesce in them, and find our happiness in the doing of His will!

I note from this narrative that we do not get rid of a responsibility by putting it out of sight. Joseph's brethren sold him into Egypt, and thought they were finally done with him. We shall see by-and-bye how grievously they misjudged. They had to confront him again, and they were held accountable for disposing of him as they did here. But how many people among ourselves act precisely as they did? They have, let us say, a troublesome son in the family, who is unsteady and unreliable in his habits, and they send him away— it makes no matter where, if only he is out of *their* sight and does not disturb *their* peace. Scarcely a week elapses that does not see some young man landed in America who has been sent away thus from his father's house on the other side of the Atlantic; and many of the families of well-to-do people have similar representatives in some of the new settlements in the West. They are sent away *just to get rid of them*. Ah! but that does not send away the responsibility, and I fear that there is a sad reckoning at last for many who have thus cut their own children adrift, and taken measures simply that they might be sent out of their sight. "Where is thy son?" may then be as hard for them to answer as Cain found that other question: "Where is thy brother?"

We may see here that there is a retributive element in our troubles. Jacob in his earlier days had deceived his father Isaac, and now his children conspire to impose upon him. He did not know at the time that they were lying to him, but, when it all came out at the last, he would, I doubt not, recognise that God in His providence was punishing him for deceiving Isaac, by letting his children deceive himself. This was one of his "chickens" that came home to "roost," and very bitter was the experience. So let us remember that we are sowing seeds in our conduct now which shall spring up and bring forth fruit after their kind in our later lives. What says the Lord Jesus? "With what measure ye mete, it shall be measured to you again." Therefore take care now how you treat other people, for you may be sure that before you get through some one else will treat you in the same way. God's providence has a retributive element in it. That is what the Psalmist refers to when he says, "With the merciful Thou wilt shew Thyself merciful; with an upright man Thou wilt shew Thyself upright; with the pure Thou wilt shew Thyself pure; and with the froward Thou wilt shew Thyself froward." Take care, therefore, how you treat others, and to this end get from Jesus Christ the spirit to act upon the golden rule, " All things whatsoever ye would that men should do unto you, do ye even so unto them; for this is the Law and the Prophets."

III.

CARRIED AWAY INTO SLAVERY.
GENESIS xxxix. 1-7.

THE Ishmaelites carried Joseph with them into Egypt, and sold him there into slavery. But as so much depends, both for the understanding of the narrative and for the vindication of its credibility, on a knowledge of the characteristics, history, and antiquities of that remarkable country, it may be well, before we follow farther the career of the young captive, that we should have some definite ideas on these important particulars. The name Egypt, in its strictest significance, belongs to the valley of the Nile from the first cataract to the Mediterranean—that is to say, between 24° 6' and 31° 36' of north latitude. The average breadth of the valley up to the bifurcation of the river at the apex of the delta is about six miles, although at certain places it widens to about sixteen. It was divided into three portions—Upper, Middle, and Lower, the Upper lying farthest to the south, the Lower to the north, and the Middle between. But the dual form of the Hebrew word which signifies Egypt seems to indicate that originally there were only two divisions, the Upper and the Lower. Bounded on the north by the sea, and on all other sides by immense deserts, the land is an oasis which depends for its fertility entirely on the annual overflow of the river; for, except in the region which borders on the Mediterranean, there is no rainfall worth mentioning, and in the southern district not a cloud

is seen in the sky all the year round. In these circumstances the extent and utilisation of the yearly flood of the
Nile involve in them the prosperity—one might almost say
the very life—of the people ; and long before the origin of
the wonderful phenomenon was known thay had learned
to turn it to the greatest advantage. For many centuries
a mystery enshrouded this periodical inundation, and the
source of the Nile was regarded as one of those secrets
which Nature refused to reveal.

Somewhere about a hundred and twenty years ago the
intrepid traveller Bruce thought that he had succeeded in
discovering it, but though the account of his adventures
was singularly interesting, and later investigators have
confirmed even the most startling of his statements, it
was ultimately found that he had mistaken one of the
tributaries of the river for its main stream, and only very
recently have the real facts in regard to the matter been
brought to light by the labours of Burton, Speke, Grant,
and Livingstone, supplemented by those of Stanley and
Baker. We now know that it is formed by the junction, at
Khartoum, in latitude 15° 35' north, of the White Nile with
the Blue Nile. The White Nile comes from the Victoria
Nyanza, a large lake situated under the equator. The Blue
Nile rises in the alpine regions of Abyssinia. After the
junction of those two main branches the river receives, in
latitude 17° 45' north, the Atbara or Black Nile, and for
the remainder of its course it runs without the addition of
another tributary. From the equatorial source of the Nile
to its mouth at the Mediterranean the length of its course
is, according to Baker, about three thousand four hundred
miles, and he says that "it may be divided into two portions
by almost halving the thirty-two degrees of latitude in a
direct line. Fifteen will include the rainy zone north of the
equator, and the remaining seventeen to Alexandria com-
prise the vast deserts which are devoid of water." Now

the explanation of the inundation is as follows: The White Nile, fed by the immense equatorial lakes, which are themselves supported by a rainfall lasting for more than nine months out of the twelve, and which constitute great natural reservoirs, sends down a constant, vast, and only slightly varying stream of water to the sea.

Unlike the White Nile, however, the Blue Nile and the Atbara tributaries are largely intermittent, and in the dry season would fail, without the White River, to reach the Mediterranean at all. On the other hand, without these two affluents the Nile would have no flood, and, even if it had, would leave little or no alluvial deposit. But the heavy summer rains in Abyssinia, which fall between May and September, wash down the rich lands of that country by the Blue Nile and the Atbara, and these, added to the ordinary current of the White Nile, increase its volume so as to cause the periodical overflow, and at the same time to charge its waters with red argillaceous mud to such an extent that when spread over a wide surface, and allowed sufficient slackness of current for the purpose, they precipitate over the land that rich alluvial dressing which enables it to produce a constant series of the most abundant harvests.

Thus, roughly speaking, the White Nile supplies the unfailing volume of water, and the Abyssinian tributaries give the annual inundation. The river begins to rise at Cairo about the end of June, and goes on increasing until the end of September, then, after remaining at the same level for a few days, it commences to fall, and continues to do so until about the middle of the following May. If the rise be less than twenty-four feet there will be a scanty harvest, and if less than twenty there will be a famine; but if it exceed thirty, the villages will be flooded, and great damage will be the result. Thus, in a very literal sense, Egypt is, as it was anciently said to be, " the gift of the Nile"; for everything in the land depends, directly or indirectly, on the river, and we cannot wonder that it became an object of reverence, if not of worship, among the people.

The inhabitants of this remarkable country very early attained to a high degree of civilisation. They were the oldest of the nations, and the first in most of the liberal arts. Jealous as the modern Chinese and Coreans of all foreigners, they had little or nothing of the station-ariness by which these hermit peoples have been distinguished, but had made great advancement in many directions. At the time of Abraham's sojourn among them they had a settled government and established laws. They had built cities and practised agriculture, and when the wealth of neighbouring communities consisted in flocks and herds, they had found out the value of real estate, and reverenced a landmark as a god. Even at that early date the great Pyramid was in existence to attest their proficiency in mechanics; and the monuments which have been disentombed in recent years, and whose inscriptions have been deciphered by modern scholars, prove that they had invented hieroglyphic writing, and were gradually advancing towards an alphabet. From the same source we learn many particulars of their manners and customs in common life, and it is interesting to note, as we shall have to do in the further consideration of the life of Joseph, the exact harmony of the descriptions given in the narrative with the delineations found upon the monuments.

Their early history is quite uncertain, and it would serve no good purpose to enter here into a detailed account of the thirty or thirty-one dynasties of kings enumerated by Manetho, or to explain the various theories which have been advanced regarding them by such men as Bunsen, Lane, Lepsius, and others. It may be enough to say that

all agree in considering that one great landmark in
Egyptian history is the invasion and dominion of the
Hyksos or Shepherd kings, and that another is the overthrow and expulsion of these usurpers.   The most eminent
authorities designate the fifteenth, sixteenth, and seventeenth dynasties as those of the Shepherds.   With the
eighteenth a new epoch was inaugurated; and as the
Pharaoh of the time of the Exodus is now by most
identified with Menepthath, son of Rameses II., of the
nineteenth dynasty, the Pharaoh of Joseph is supposed to
be one of the kings of the seventeenth dynasty, whose date
is in the later part of the Shepherd dominion, and somewhat before B.C. 1700.

Joseph would thus be raised to his position as governor
of Egypt by a king who, though himself a foreigner, was
one of those who had, as the result of the long sojourn of
his people in the land, adopted Egyptian titles and usages,
and the king, "who knew not Joseph," may have belonged
to the new dynasty by whom the Shepherds were expelled.
This is the view—in the main, at least—adopted by Poole,
who thus writes: "The story of Joseph is illustrated step
by step from the Egyptian texts.   The 'Tale of the Two
Brothers,' the earliest known of Egyptian fictions, was no
sooner read than it was seen to relate, in its turning-point,
an incident identical with the trial of Joseph.   Pharaoh's
dream of the kine describes the years of plenty and famine
under the usual type of the inundation, as Dr. Birch has
shown.   The installation of Joseph has its parallel in the
case of an Egyptian governor of the age of the eighteenth
dynasty, who received exactly the same office, 'Lord of
all Egypt,'* in the Egyptian record a 'lord of the whole
land,' the word lord being '*adon*' in both cases.†   The
term in Hebrew means 'ruler'; in Egyptian its sense is

---

* Gen. xlv. 9.   † Brugsch, "History," i. 269, 270.

more special, and the whole title of Joseph may best be
rendered 'regent.'*   Two circumstances of the narrative
bring us very near Egyptian official usages. 'By the
life of Pharaoh' is used as a strong asseveration by
Joseph,† and when he has sworn to his father, after the
Hebrew manner, that he will not bury him in Egypt, then
'Israel bowed himself upon the head of his staff.' ‡   Both
the expression 'by the life of Pharaoh' and the custom of
bowing upon the staff of an officer are traced by M. Chabas
in his interesting essays on Egyptian judicial proceedings,
where he cites the following passage describing the taking
an oath by a witness in a trial at Thebes: 'He made a
life of the royal lord, striking his nose and his ears, and
placing himself on the head of the staff,'§ the ordinary
oath when the witness bowed himself on the magistrate's
staff of office. He well remarks that this explains the
passage in Genesis quoted as above, as a recognition by
Jacob of his son's authority.‖   This illustration shows
the Septuagint is right in reading *hamatteh* staff, in
agreement with Hebrews xi. 71, where the Masoretes
read *hamittah* bed, and a question of controversy disappears."   Then, after a most interesting series of para-
graphs on the oppression of the Israelites in Egypt, and
their exodus out of it, he proceeds in this wise: "The
date of the Hebrew documents in general has been here
assumed to be that assigned to them by the older scholars.
This position is justified by the Egyptian evidence.
German and Dutch critics have laboured with extraordinary acuteness and skill upon the Mosaic documents alone, with such illustrations as they could
obtain from collateral records, using, be it remembered,
such records as all the older and too many of the later

---

* "Brugsch," *l. c.*   † Gen. xii. 15, 16.   ‡ Gen. xlvii. 29-31.
§ "Mélange's Egyptologiques," iii. I. 80.   ‖ *Ibid*, 91, 92.

classical scholars out of Germany and France have used coins and inscriptions, not as independent sources, but as mere illustrations. The work has been that of great literary critics, not of archæologists. The result has been to reduce the date of the documents, except a few fragments, by many centuries. [But] the Egyptian documents emphatically call for a reconsideration of the whole question of the date of the Pentateuch.

It is now certain that the narrative of the history of Joseph and the sojourn and exodus of the Israelites—that is to say, the portion from Genesis xxxix. to Exodus xv.—so far as it relates to Egypt, is substantially not much later than B.C. 1300; in other words, was written while the memory of the events was fresh. The minute accuracy of the text is inconsistent with any later date. It is not merely that it shows knowledge of Egypt, but knowledge of Egypt under the Ramessides, and yet earlier. The condition of the country, the chief cities of the frontier, the composition of the army, are true of the age of the Ramessides and not true of the age of the Pharaohs, contemporary with Solomon and his successors.

If the Hebrew documents are of the close of the period of the kings of Judah, how is it that they are true of the earlier condition, not of that which was contemporary with those kings? Why is the Egypt of the Law markedly different from the Egypt of the Prophets, each condition being described consistently with its Egyptian records, themselves contemporary with the events? Why is Egypt described in the Law as one kingdom, and no hint given of the break-up of the Empire into the small principalities mentioned by Isaiah (xix. 2)? Why do the proper names belong to the Ramesside, and earlier age, without a single instance of those Semitic names which came into fashion with the Bubastic line in Solomon's time? Why do Zoan-Rameses and Zoar take the places of Migdol and

Tahpanhes? Why are the foreign mercenaries, such as
the Lubrin, spoken of in the constitution of Egyptian
armies in the time of the kingdom of Judah, wholly unmentioned? The relations of Egypt with foreign countries
are not less characteristic. The kingdom of Ethiopia,
which overshadowed Egypt from before Hezekiah's time
and throughout his reign, is unmentioned in the earlier
documents. The earlier Assyrian Empire, which rose for
a time on the fall of the Egyptian, nowhere appears.

"These agreements have not failed to strike foreign
Egyptologists who have no theological bias. These
independent scholars, without actually formulating any
view of the date of the greater part of the Pentateuch,
appear uniformly to treat its text as an authority to be
cited side by side with the Egyptian monuments. So
Lepsius, in his researches on the date of the Exodus, and
Brugsch, in his discussion of the route, and Chabas, in
his paper on Rameses and Pithan. Of course it would be
unfair to implicate any one of these scholars in the
inferences expressed above; but, at the same time, it is
impossible that they can, for instance, hold Kuenen's
theories of the date of the Pentateuch, so far as the part
relating to Egypt is concerned. They have taken the two
sets of documents—Hebrew and Egyptian—side by side,
and in the working of elaborate problems found everything
consistent with accuracy on both sides; and, of course,
accuracy would not be maintained in a tradition handed
down through several centuries. If the large portion of
the Pentateuch relating to the Egyptian period of Hebrew
history, including as it does Elohistic as well as Jehovistic
sections, is of the remote antiquity here claimed for it, no
one can doubt that the first four books of Moses are
substantially of the same age." *

---

* Reginald Stuart Poole, art. MODERN EGYPT, in *Contemporary
Review*, March, 1879, pp. 752, 753, 757-59.

I make no apology for the length of this quotation; its own excellence is my best defence. But I wish you to bear in mind in connection with it the following particulars: In the first place, it is the deliberate judgment, given not much more than six years ago in the pages of the *Contemporary Review*, of one who is regarded as a competent authority on the matters to which he refers. He was selected to write the article on Egypt in Smith's "Dictionary of the Bible." He is joint author with a coadjutor of his own name of the article on Egypt in the new edition of the "Encyclopædia Britannica"; so that what he says on Egyptology must command respectful attention. In the second place, he is of necessity also a good scholar in Hebrew and the cognate languages, able to appreciate and to weigh in the balance of an independent and well-informed judgment the statements of the Higher Critics in their own department. In the third place, he has no prejudice against the Higher Critics as such. So far from that being the case, he speaks of them in terms of the greatest respect, and rightly warns those who accept his conclusions from rushing to the extreme of denying altogether the value of criticism; while, at the same time, he clearly sees that, as presently cultivated, its excellences in analysis are marred by its defects in constructive skill. He thus occupies impartial ground, being neither trammelled by authority nor enslaved by specialism. Then, in the fourth place, his judgment is given without any hesitation in behalf of the received date of the first four books of the Pentateuch and their historical credibility.

It has come to be regarded, I know not why, that scholarship is altogether on the side of those who would have us to look upon the earliest books of Scripture as so many collections of myths, or sagas, or the like; and every one who raises his voice against such opinions is held, *ipso facto*, to be an ignoramus, altogether incompetent to pronounce an opinion on the subject. Moreover, they who advocate the theories of Kuenen, and others of the same school, are heralded as reformers, new Martin Luthers, who have come to usher in a grander liberty than the great German dreamed of; and their words are caught by the swift fingers of the reporters for the press, and sent all over the land, while utterances like those which I have just quoted are allowed to fall to the ground unheeded; though perhaps it may be found that in the end liberty will be better served by adhering to the old than by following the new. But new or old is not the question; liberty or not is not the question. The question is, *True* or *not?* and on that issue I would give a thousand times more weight to the judgment of a competent and candid expert like Reginald Stuart Poole than to that of a mere retailer of the destructive conclusions of the most recent rationalistic critics.

And now, having once for all disposed of this subject, let us look very briefly at Joseph's first position in Egypt. It was that of a slave exposed for sale in the open market. God be thanked, we can now repeat these words without the humiliating consciousness that a similar sight might still be seen within our own borders! It was a pitiful plight to be in—to have to face the peering looks of possible purchasers, as they scanned the special " points " that were noteworthy in him; to hear the tones of criticisms that were otherwise unintelligible; and to be led away at length by one who called him his property. Oh! it is too horrible to think of! One's whole manhood rises up in rebellion against the very idea; and we would have excused Joseph if he had manifested some resistance on the occasion. For God has given me to myself, and no mortal has a right to me as a chattel. If Tell was a hero because he fought against the tyranny of Austria;

and Bruce because he struggled against the oppression of England; and Washington because he rebelled against the injustice of Great Britain—is not the slave also a hero who struggles for his personal liberty? What right has a nation to its autonomy more than a man has to his freedom? And if we honour the soldier who helps an oppressed people to independence, shall we not honour also him who helps a slave to freedom? These were the sentiments that animated John Brown in his famous expedition; and, though it was at first a failure, it proved in the end to have been a splendid success.

But there was no one near poor Joseph to help him into liberty, and so he was bought and led away by Potiphar, an officer of Pharaoh and "captain of the guard." He is called an Egyptian, probably to mark that while his master was one of the Shepherd kings, he himself belonged to a native family; and this view is supported by the fact that his name contains that of an Egyptian divinity. He is styled "the captain of the guard," or, as the original may be more literally rendered, "chief of the executioners." It is not easy to say what office that title specially designated. Some would make it "chief-marshal," others, "provost-marshal," and others "master of the horse." Dr. Kitto considers it to be "chief of the royal police." He writes as follows: "Potiphar was undoubtedly the chief of the executioners; but this is a high office in the East as a *court* office, for such executioners have nothing to do with the execution of the awards of the law, in its ordinary course, but only with those of the king. It is thus an office of great responsibility; and, to insure its proper and, if need be, prompt execution, it is entrusted to an officer of the court, who has necessarily under his command a body of men whose duty it is to preserve the order and peace of the palace and its precincts, to attend and guard the

royal person on public occasions, and under the direction
of their chief to inflict such punishment as the king awards
upon those who incur his displeasure. He therefore, in
this sense, may be called 'captain of the guard' or
'chief-marshal.' Further, it appears that this officer
had, adjoining to or connected with his house, a round
building in which the king's prisoners—those who had
incurred the royal suspicion or displeasure—were detained
in custody till their doom should be determined. A
functionary who combined these various duties in his
person cannot perhaps be better described than by the
title, 'chief of the royal police.'" *

When he saw his destination, Joseph, rightly believing
that he was still the ward of Jehovah, determined to
accept the situation, and adjust himself to his environment. Therefore he did willingly, and with his best skill,
everything that was required at his hands; so that he
soon secured the confidence of his master, who found it
to be to his interest to intrust everything in his establishment to Joseph's care. "He left all that he had in
Joseph's hand; and he knew not aught he had, save the
bread which he did eat." This is quite in harmony with
what we know otherwise of the custom of the time; for
the Egyptian monuments frequently represent scribes or
stewards as superintending the property of rich men, and
carefully registering all the operations of the household,
the garden, the field, &c. Joseph did all this so well
that everything went on with harmony and turned out
profitably, and Potiphar congratulated himself that he
had got a treasure in his slave. Joseph, too, might be
rejoicing within himself that the lines had fallen unto him
in such pleasant places, and contrasting his lot with that

---

* Kitto's "Bible History of the Holy Land," quoted in Fairbairn's
"Imperial Bible Dictionary," art. POTIPHAR.

of many a poor slave in the land, when, through the very
loyalty of his heart to his master, and the very strictness
of his adherence to the course of purity and rectitude,
he found himself at length consigned as a criminal to
prison. How all that came about, and what ultimately
resulted from it, will appear as we proceed. Meanwhile
we must here break off, and linger only long enough to
take with us two or three practical lessons, which may
help us under and through the captivities of our lives.

We have all our captivities at some time or other in our
experience. The essence of Joseph's trial here was that
he was taken whither he had no wish to go, and was
prevented from going back again to the home in which
his father was sitting mourning for his loss. But is not
interference with our comfort or our liberty still the bitter
element in all our afflictions? Take bodily illness, for
example, and when you get at the root of the discomfort
of it you find it in the union of these two things : you are
where you do not want to be—where you would never
have thought of putting yourself—and you are held there,
whether you will or not, by a Power that is stronger than
your own. No external force constrains you, no fetters
are on your limbs, yet you are held where you are against
your own liking, and you do not relish the situation—you
are a captive. But the same thing comes out in almost
every sort of trial. You are, let me suppose, in business
perplexity. But that is not of your own choosing ; if you
could have managed it you would have been in quite different circumstances. Yet, in spite of you, things have
gone against you. Men whom you had implicitly trusted,
and whom you would have had no more thought of doubting than you would think now of doubting your mother's
love, have proved deceitful ; or the course of trade has
gone against you, and you are brought to a stand. You
have been carried away perhaps by brothers, perhaps by

Ishmaelites—for the race is not yet extinct—from the Canaan of comfort to the Egypt of captivity, and you are now in helpless perplexity. It may be standing not, like Joseph, in the slave-pen, but in the market-place of labour, aud condemned to do nothing, because "no man hath hired" you. There are many in a large city who are in just such circumstances. What then? Let them learn from Joseph that the first thing to do in a captivity is to acquiesce in it as the will of God concerning them.

The young Israelite did not lose time or strength by struggling unwisely against a higher might than his own; he bowed to the inevitable, and adjusted himself to it, because he had learned, from his talks with his good old grandfather Isaac and his father Jacob, that God was in it, and had a watchful eye over his history. So in a trial we have, first of all, to accept it as the will of God in Christ Jesus concerning us, and to say regarding it, "This also cometh from the Lord, who is wonderful in council and excellent in working." Fretting over that from which we have been removed, or which has been taken away from us, will not make things better, but it will prevent us from improving those which remain. The bond is only tightened by our stretching it to the uttermost. The impatient horse which will not quietly endure his halter only strangles himself in his stall. The high-mettled animal that is restive in the yoke only galls his shoulders; and every one will understand the difference between the restless starling of which Sterne has written, breaking its wings against the bars of its cage, and crying, "I can't get out! I can't get out!" and the docile canary that sits upon its perch and sings as if it would outrival the lark at heaven's own gate, so moving its mistress to open the door of its prison-house and give it the full range of the room. He who is constantly looking back and bewailing what he has lost does only thereby unfit himself for improving in any way the discipline to which God has subjected him; whereas the man who brings his mind down to his lower lot, and deliberately examines how he can serve God best in that, is already on his way to better things. Thus, paradoxical as it may seem, acquiescence in an affliction is the first step in the way out of it.

But then, we must learn from Joseph to make the best of our remaining opportunities in our captivity. If he was to be a slave, Joseph was determined he would be the best of slaves, and what he was required to do he would do with his might and with his heart. This is a most important consideration, and it may, perhaps, help to explain why similar trials have had such different results in different persons. One has been bemoaning that it is not with him as it used to be, while the other has discovered that some talents have been still left him, and he has set to work with these. One has been saying, " If I had only the resources which I once possessed I could do something ; but now they have gone, I am helpless." But the other has been soliloquizing thus : " If I can do nothing else I can at least do this, little as it is ; and if I put it into the hand of Christ, He can make it great "; and so we account for the unhappiness and uselessness of the one, and for the happiness and usefulness of the other. Nor will it do to say that this difference is a mere thing of temperament. It is a thing of character. The one acts in faith, recognising God's hand in his affliction, the other acts in unbelief, seeing nothing but his own calamity, and that only increases his affliction. So we come to this : keep fast hold of God's hand in your captivity, and do your best in that which is open to you. That will ultimately bring you out of it ; but if you lose that you will lose everything.

IV.

TEMPTED BUT TRIUMPHANT.

Genesis xxxix. 7-23.

WE have no absolutely certain data from which to make a calculation; but as Joseph is said to have been thirty years of age when he first stood before Pharaoh; * as two years elapsed after his interpretation of the dreams of the chief butler and the chief baker before he was sent for to explain those of the king; † and as some little time must be allowed—say, at least, one year—for his rise from a prisoner to the office of chief warden in the prison, this would make him twenty-seven at the beginning of his imprisonment. Now he was seventeen when he was first sold into the hands of the Ishmaelites, ‡ and so we get the result, conjectural indeed, but yet probable, that he served in the house of Potiphar for ten years. During all that time he had given the highest satisfaction to his master, and, at length, had so grown into his confidence that, except in the preparation of his food—a matter which no Egyptian would intrust to a foreigner—Potiphar had left the management of his affairs entirely in his hands. But now there came a terrible trial, before which multitudes would have fallen, but out of which he came blighted, indeed, for a season in reputation, but strengthened and ennobled in character, and so the better fitted for the performance of the work which

---

* Gen. xli. 46.   † Gen. xli. 1.   ‡ Gen. xxxvii. 2.

he had still to do. The particulars of that trial are set forth with sufficient distinctness in the narrative, and need not be dwelt on here. Suffice it to say that the wife of his master sought to make him partner with herself in a guilty intrigue, which had in it some strong elements of allurement to a young man of his age and in his circumstances. I say nothing now of the shameless immorality of his temptress, except to remark that it is quite in keeping with some representations of Egyptian women which have been found upon the recently discovered frescoes. For though now, in all Eastern lands, women are secluded and kept in harems by themselves, the Egyptian females of those early times were not only under no particular restraint, but were sometimes addicted to excesses. Thus, Wilkinson tells us that they were not restricted in the use of wine and in the enjoyment of other luxuries, and that "the painters, in illustrating this fact, have sometimes sacrificed their gallantry to a love of caricature. Some call the servants to support them as they sit, others with difficulty prevent themselves from falling on those behind them ; a basin is brought too late by a reluctant servant ; and the faded flower which is ready to drop from their heated hands is intended to be characteristic of their own sensations."* A description like that may enable us, perhaps, the better to understand the statements made in the sacred history.

But leaving such gross and repulsive things, let us look at the magnitude of this temptation. It came on Joseph when he was dwelling among a nation of idolaters, away from the restraints of home and the influence of his father and grandfather, by which he had been accustomed to be regulated. If, therefore, his piety had been a mere conventional thing, he would certainly have yielded, as many

---

* "The Manners and Customs of the Ancient Egyptians," by Sir J. G. Wilkinson, vol. i.

others in like circumstances have done. Which of us has
not known cases of youths who at home were reputable
and well behaved, but who, when they have gone to
another city or another land, where they were entirely
unknown to those by whom they were surrounded, have
run riot in iniquity, and excused themselves by quoting the
debasing proverb that " when we are in Rome we must do
as they do at Rome " ? But Joseph was not a youth of
that sort. His piety was not a matter of longitude and
latitude. He believed in God, and sought to serve Him in
all places and in all cases ; and he did in Egypt precisely
as he would have done, in like circumstances, in Canaan.

Again, this temptation, which came upon him thus when
he was away from all external support, took him in two
points of his nature at one and the same time. It
appealed to appetite ; and if Paul thought it needful to
say to Timothy, who was a young man of rather ascetic
habits, devoted to the ministry of the gospel, and surrounded by all wholesome influences, " flee also youthful
lusts," we may well believe that Joseph was not insen-
sible to its force in that particular. But that was not its
most seductive aspect, as I believe, to him. For the
entering into this intrigue meant also for him the putting
of Potiphar ultimately out of the way, and his own elevation, in an easy and speedy fashion, to his master's
place. That must be clear to all acquainted with Eastern
life. Now see what all that implied. Joseph had not forgotten his early dreams. There still hovered before him
a vision of the time when his brothers should make
obeisance to him, and he should rise to some post of
dignity and influence on the earth—the hope of attaining
that upheld him all those years—and lo ! here is a short
and alluring pathway to what seemed to promise that very
thing. Might he not take it, therefore, without reluctance
or compunction ? Thus there came upon him at once two

of the very allurements which Satan put, one after the
other, before the Lord Jesus in the wilderness. You
remember that to the hungry Son of Man the tempter
said, "If Thou be the Son of God, command that these
stones be made bread," thereby opening the door for the
satisfaction of appetite in a forbidden way ; and again,
that to Him who came into the world to be a King whose
dominion should be universal, he said on the mountain-
top, after he had shown Him all the kingdoms of the world
and the glory of them, "All these will I give Thee if Thou
wilt fall down and worship me," thus offering Him the
crown without the cross, and the long and arduous journey
that led up thereto.   Now, precisely these were the temptations that Joseph here had to face. They took the Lord,
as I have said, one after the other ; but they came upon
Joseph both at once, and he had to meet them without
having the advantage of the armoury of the written word
wherein Jesus found the weapons with which He repulsed
His adversary. But just as little would he yield as did the
Lord.   It was not that there was in him no fleshly
appetite, but that he had learned to keep that in its place,
and to make it subservient to the service of his God.   It
was not that he had no ambition, but that he was content
to wait for its gratification until that could be secured in
a manner worthy of his God's approval.   And so he put
them both from him with no half-hearted opposition, but
in a decided and determined manner.   There was no
"yes" in the "no" which he uttered, and when he was
assailed with repeated importunity, he only repeated more
emphatically his refusal.

Nor can we help remarking on the grounds whereon he
based his conduct, for they show as really his fidelity to
man as his loyalty to God. He could not be guilty of
treachery against Potiphar, or of sin against God. His
own pleasure or elevation would be too dearly purchased

by ingratitude to one who had placed such unlimited confidence in him, and no gratification could to him be lasting which dishonoured God.

But after he had taken that stand, and by the very taking of it, he made an implacable enemy of his mistress. One of our greatest poets has spoken of " lust hard by hate," and another has affirmed that

" Hell hath no fury like a woman scorned,"

so that we do not wonder at the course which she followed. She was determined to ruin him, one way or another, and therefore when, to get rid of her solicitations, he fled from her, leaving his garment in her hand, she immediately saw her opportunity for revenge, and went to her husband with the cunningly woven story which is thus given in the record : " The Hebrew servant which thou hast brought unto us, came in unto me to mock me ; and it came to pass, as I lifted up my voice and cried, that he left his garment with me and fled out." The result was that Potiphar, without giving Joseph an opportunity to vindicate himself, put him at once into the king's prison ; or, as the words literally rendered are, " the house of roundness," "the round house where the king's prisoners were bound." This is described by Kitto as " an edifice or portion of the official mansion, mostly subterranean, of which the roof or vault, rising immediately from the surface of the ground, was round or shaped like an inverted bowl. That it was of this nature may be inferred from its being called in chapter xli. 15, the 'dungeon.' " He adds that " such dungeons are still, under similar circumstances, used in the East, and they have usually an aperture at the top by which some light and air are admitted, and through which the prisoners are let down. They are always upon the premises of the chief of the guard or of the magistrate."*

---

* " Daily Bible Illustrations," vol. i. p. 382.

Into such a place, then, Joseph was thrust; and it is probable that at first he was treated with much harshness, for we are told in the hundred and fifth Psalm* that "they hurt his feet with fetters and laid him in irons." It was very sad, but it might have been worse; and it would have been worse if he had been there and guilty; but as he was there and guiltless, he could still look up to God, and take a silent appeal to Him. For a time, indeed, he may have been utterly cast down; but at length he found his old consolation in his religious faith, and by his demeanour he so won upon his jailer that the rigour of his confinement was relaxed, and he became the trusted servant of the keeper of the prison, who committed to him the care of all who had been intrusted to his custody.

But here we must leave him for a while, and turn aside from the course of the history to gather up some wholesome lessons from the portion of it which has at this time been under our review.

We may learn, then, that when we have unusual blessing we may look for severe temptation. Joseph had been preferred to great honour. His master intrusted everything to his care, and he had reached a position of ease and comfort and respectability. There was much in all this prosperity to lull him into sleep, as if now he had passed through the dangerous stage in his career; yet out of that very prosperity came this new peril, and it was the greatest which he had yet encountered. For though his brothers had sold him into slavery, they could not and did not dispose of his soul; but this was a temptation to sell his soul into the slavery of sin. It is sometimes suggested, by the way in which men speak of affliction and adversity, that these are the only experiences which are fraught with peril to the character. But I believe that there is more

---

* Verse 18.

real risk in prosperity than in either of the others, and I
know that in the Scriptures this is very strikingly illustrated by many sad examples.   David stood well all the
tests of privation and persecution when he was on the way
to the throne, but after he had reached it, and had sur-
mounted all his difficulties, he fell into heinous sin.   And
if we care to look around us, we shall discover that the
critical times in the history of many men have not been
while they were struggling up the hill in self-help, but
after they had reached the summit.   It takes a steady
hand to carry a full cup ; it requires a good head to stand
upon a lofty height ; and those who have got as high as
they can reach—who are, as we say, at the top of
the tree—had need be on their guard lest some Delilah
should come to worm out of them the secret of their
strength, and deliver them over as captives to the Prince
of Darkness.   The more prosperous you are, therefore, the nearer you are to the top in your profession or
business, seek to be the more watchful, for in the spiritual
warfare, as in that of earth, " eternal vigilance is the price
of safety."

But we may learn from this history, that when temptation takes us we must resist it with a strong and decided
" No," and carefully take ourselves out of its range. Joseph
put the matter on the highest ground when he said, " How
can I do this great wickedness and sin against God?" and
he held no parley with his temptress, but steadily refused
her importunity, and finally ran away from her presence.
This course, though it roused her indignation, yet kept
himself from defilement, and stands in striking contrast to
that followed, for example, by Samson.   If that singularly
weak man, for all so strong as he was, had never entered
into conversation with Delilah about his strength, he had
never lost it and fallen a victim to the Philistines. If he
had not allowed her to weave the seven locks of his hair

into a web, he had not ultimately told her wherein his strength did really lie. But by little and little, through his parley with her, he gave himself into her power. So, again, when Balaam said " No" to Balak, he did so in such a half-hearted way as to reveal that he would much rather have said " Yes," and therefore, when the application was renewed, he went on in that way which ended in destruction. Now, there must be no such half-heartedness with us. Let us say " No " to sin as if we meant it—not rudely, indeed, for there is no need for rudeness, but distinctly and decidedly, like those whose minds have been made up to the course to which they mean to adhere. And if the application be repeated, let us repeat our refusal, if possible, more emphatically than ever. When Nehemiah was assailed by his adversaries, who sought to beguile him into the plain of Ono, that they might there assassinate him, he replied, " I am doing a great work, and I cannot come down. Why should the work cease while I leave it and come down to you ? " And when they sent to him four times after this sort, he answered them as many times after the same manner. So let it be with us. Let our " Nay " here be unmistakable, without any qualification, or reservation, or apology, and then, if after all it is not thoroughly understood, let us run away, as Joseph did, even though we should leave our raiment behind us, believing, as Matthew Henry quaintly says, that " it is better to lose a good coat than a good conscience." Ah ! how many there are who go out to court a temptation. Heedless of the command of Christ, " Watch and pray, lest ye enter into temptation," they deliberately put themselves in its way, and of course they fall before it. That result is just about as certain as it is that there will be an explosion if, with an open barrel of gunpowder in your arms, you go into a smithy where the sparks are flying all around. " Can a man take fire into his bosom and his

clothes not be burned? Can one go upon hot coals and
his feet not be burned?" No more can you put yourself
into the way of temptation without injuring your souls.
It would be perilous to do so, even if you were innocent
and holy; how much more so, considering the inherent
depravity by which we are all characterised! It is
dangerous to drive restive horses near the edge of a
precipice; it is dangerous to bring gunpowder near the
fire; it is dangerous to come near an adder's fangs; and
it is equally so with these fallen natures of ours to
approach temptation. Therefore " avoid it, pass not by it,
turn from it and pass away."

But the merely negative attitude will, after all, be weak,
and so I stay here a moment longer to add that the best
means of saying " No " to sin is to say " Yes " with the
whole heart to the Lord Jesus Christ. If you wish to
dispel the darkness you will bring in a light; if you desire
to kill weeds most effectively you will sow the ground
with wholesome grass; and, in like manner, if you would
keep evil out of your hearts you must get the Lord Jesus
Christ into them. You all know what affection for, and
trust in, a person have done in common life to produce
prompt decision and persistent action. Every scholar
remembers the instance of that true wife, Penelope, who
for long years turned away suitors for her hand, and was
ultimately rewarded by the return of Ulysses, who had
manifested a constancy and affection that were equal to
her own. Now, if in domestic life such effects are produced by these two principles, love and trust—which are
not so much two as one working in two different ways—
may we not believe that, by the grace of the Holy Spirit,
personal attachment to the Lord Jesus Christ, and implicit
trust in Him, will give us quickness of sight to see what He
would have us to do, and firmness of purpose to do that
with our might? Nothing is so clear-sighted as love. It

is on the alert at the approach of the slightest danger; and if only we take care to continue in the love of Christ, that will keep us right, for it will reveal the tempter to us even under his most cunning disguise, and give us courage and firmness to withstand him. Nay, more, let us but have the love of Christ strong within us, and we shall not think that there is anything like a sacrifice or a hardship in saying " No " to sin, for we shall have no hankering after that which He disapproves. Our refusal to sin will be then only the outworking of our satisfaction with Him; the consequence of our delight in Him, and not the result of any outward compulsion. Here, young man, is the key to the whole position: fill the heart with Christ, and when the tempter comes he will find it so pre-occupied that there is no room in it for him and his seduction.

But we may learn from this history that we should not be surprised to find that our adherence to the right is followed at first by great hardship. Poor Joseph! what must he have thought when he found himself in the dungeon? Had God forgotten him? If not, how came he to be in such a miserable plight? Was there any God at all? If so, how was such treatment of an innocent man consistent with rectitude? Would it not have been better for him to have yielded and taken the short cut to affluence and ease? To what end should he make a point of resisting temptation if the temptress continues to enjoy her luxury, and the innocent resister of her will is cast into a dungeon? Ah! this is the very trial in a trial when it tempts us to distrust God, or to think that He has forsaken us; and it may be that Joseph felt it keenly for a season, even as it was felt by the author of the seventy-third Psalm and the sweet singer of the thirty-seventh. Admirably has one said here, " It is this which has made the world seem so terrible a place to many—that the innocent must so often suffer for the guilty, and that without appeal the pure and loving must lie in chains and bitterness, while the wicked live and see good days. It is this that has made men most despairingly question whether there be, indeed, a God in heaven who knows who the real culprit is, and yet suffers a terrible doom slowly to close around the innocent; who sees where the guilt lies, and yet moves no finger nor speaks the word that would bring justice to light, shaming the secure triumph of the wrong-doer, and saving the bleeding spirit from its agony. It was this that came as the last stroke of the Passion of our Lord, that He was numbered among the transgressors; it was this that caused, or materially increased, the feeling that God had deserted Him; and it was this that wrung from Him the cry which once was wrung from David, and may well have been wrung from Joseph, when, cast into the dungeon as a mean and treacherous villain, whose freedom was the peril of domestic peace and honour, he found himself again help-less and forlorn, regarded now not as a mere worthless lad, but as a criminal of the lowest type. And as there always recur cases in which exculpation is impossible, just in proportion as the party accused is possessed of honourable feeling, and where silent acceptance of doom is the result, not of convicted guilt, but of the very triumph of self-sacrifice, we must beware of over-suspicion and injustice." *

But when we find ourselves in such circumstances, what is to be done? Nothing, but wait God's time and per-severe in our integrity. We must not judge God for what we see of His providence on a small scale. We must take wide views of it, and when we do that we shall find that *in the long run* He brings forth men's righteousness as the light and their judgment as the noonday, so that the evil-

---

* Marcus Dods, D.D.: " Isaac, Jacob, and Joseph," pp. 176, 177.

doer is punished and the virtuous man rewarded. And even if in some cases we should not see that, we must widen our view still further and take in eternity; then, understanding the end of the wicked, we shall not begrudge them the little time during which on earth they enjoy their good things. But, more than all, we must get above the merely utilitarian view of things, and adhere to the right because it is the right, not simply because it is the profitable. I desire to give especial emphasis to this last consideration, since, as it seems to me, there is a strong disposition among many in these days to test everything by profit. Thus we have the question pressed on our attention, "Is life worth living?" as if it were a mere question of gain; whereas the right is an eternal and immutable thing, and is to be adhered to at whatsoever sacrifice, just because it is right. There is no profit like a good conscience, and no reward equal to the approbation of God. It were well, therefore, if some of our would-be moralists to-day had as much clearness of perception on these subjects as the great Scottish novelist, who thus writes in his final introduction to "Ivanhoe": "The character of the fair Jewess found so much favour in the eyes of some fair readers that the writer was censured because, when arranging the fates of the characters of the drama, he had not assigned the hand of Wilfred to Rebecca, rather than the less interesting Rowena. But, not to mention that the prejudices of the age rendered such a union almost impossible, the author may, in passing, observe that he thinks a character of a highly virtuous nature degraded rather than exalted by an attempt to reward virtue with temporal prosperity. Such is not the recompense which Providence has deemed worthy of suffering merit; and it is a fatal doctrine to teach young persons, the most common readers of romance, that rectitude of conduct and of principle are either naturally allied with, or adequately rewarded by, the gratification of our passions or the attainment of our wishes. In a word, if a virtuous and self-denied character is dismissed with temporal wealth, greatness, rank, or the indulgence of such a rashly-formed passion as that of Rebecca for Ivanhoe, the reader will be apt to say, verily virtue has had its reward. But a glance on the great picture of life will show that the duties of self-denial and the sacrifice of passion to principle are seldom thus remunerated, and that the internal consciousness of their high-minded discharge of duty produces on their own reflections a more adequate recompense in the form of that peace which the world cannot give or take away." The upshot of it all, then, is that we must adhere to the right for its own sake, irrespective of what may be the consequence of our doing so; that, as Faber says, we should be willing "to lose with God," because we can see that "He is on the field when He is most invisible," and that we should still hold fast our conviction that

> Right is right, since God is God,
> And right the day must win;
> To doubt would be disloyalty,
> To falter would be sin.

Not for what we can make by it, or for what it is worth, but for what it is, and for its relationship to God, let us do the right, and we may rest assured, however it may be now, that in the end we shall be on the winning side. We may have to go through a prison to the final issue, or we may need to step up to it from a cross, but we shall be on the winning side, for character is success—not position, not prosperity, not reputation—but character, and *it* is made and hardened and tempered in the fire of trial. When Joseph stepped out of the prison into the chariot of the ruler over all the land of Egypt, it seemed a sudden rise, but it was in reality only a revelation of the greatness which had already shown itself in his inflexible adherence to purity before the severest temptation. Leave the reputation and the success, then, to look after themselves, and be not disconcerted if they should both be for a time under a cloud ; but look well to the CHARACTER, for that is the main thing, and the life that secures that for Christ is always worth living.

———————————

V.

THE TWO PRISONERS.

GENESIS XL.

WHILE Joseph was in charge of the royal prison, under the direction of its principal keeper, two officers of the court were consigned to his custody by the captain of the guard. This last-named dignitary was either Potiphar or his successor in office. We have, however, no hint of any change, and so, perhaps, we may conclude that Joseph's master had come to look more favourably upon him, and was glad of an opportunity of showing that he had confidence in him. One is almost inclined to believe that he had become convinced of his servant's innocence of the offence with which he had been charged; and though, in that case, it would have been simply right for Potiphar to have set him at liberty, we can well understand how the exposure which such an act would have made kept him from taking any steps in that direction; while he might be well enough pleased at seeing the mitigation of his sufferings which had resulted from his elevation to a wardenship.

The court officials who were intrusted to his care are called in the Authorised Version "the chief butler" and "the chief baker," but these titles give us no adequate idea of the dignity of the positions which they occupied. Literally rendered, the phrases are, "the chief of the cup-bearers" and "the chief of the cooks." The first of these held an office of great importance, which gave him the ear of the monarch even in his most unbending moments, and thus enabled him to exercise great influence with him. We see something of its value at a later date in the case of Nehemiah, who held a similar position in the palace of Artaxerxes; and in that of Rabshakeh, whose very name implies that he stood in the same relation to the King of Assyria. The duty of this officer was to present the cup to the king after having tasted a portion of its contents, and so made sure that they were not poisoned; but his facilities for intercourse with the monarch made him particularly sought after by interested parties as a mediator between them and the king, and so he was apt to be mixed up with all manner of cabals and intrigues. The "chief of the cooks," again, superintended the preparation of the king's food. We saw that Potiphar, much as he had trusted Joseph, would not allow even him to meddle with his food, and from that little incident we may learn how implicit must have been the confidence of the monarch in this official. Wilkinson has given a long and elaborate account of the preparation and serving of an Egyptian dinner, gleaned from the paintings on the monuments, but it would serve no good purpose to reproduce it here. Suffice it to say, that the kitchen in all its departments was directly and immediately under the care of him who is called in this history "the chief baker."

The particular crime which was laid to the charge of these two officials is not specified, though some have conjectured that it was an attempt to poison the king, and the fact that they had both to do with the supply of his table gives at least plausibility to the opinion. But from the punishment which ultimately fell upon the chief baker we may be sure that it was of an aggravated character, and probably it involved an attempt of some description on the monarch's life. In any case, they were in such suspense as to their fate that their anxiety gave a direction to their dreams; and one morning both of them awoke with a peculiarly vivid recollection of what they had seen in their dreams, and a profound impression that there was some special significance in their visions. Indeed, they had the feeling that if they could only get the interpretation of them they would have in that the revelation of what was before them. Nor was this idea altogether unnatural, for among all nations at that time, and for long after, it was generally believed that dreams were media through which divine communications were made, and in all great centres of influence there were men of recognised learning whose special office it was to explain the meaning of such visions. Homer, in a well-known passage, says that a dream is from Jupiter; and elsewhere he relates how the mind of Jove was communicated to Agamemnon in a vision. I do not imagine, indeed, that every dream was counted worthy of attention, but when the impression produced by a dream was one that could not be shaken off, we can readily understand that some special significance would be connected with it, and that it would be regarded as a Divine revelation. We cannot affirm that this view was always right, but that it was sometimes correct is evident from the cases before us, as well as from those of Pharaoh and Nebuchadnezzar; and even yet it is a question very difficult to answer in a definite manner, whether any significance, or, if any, how much, is to be attributed to any of the visions of the night. We all allow that God may and does influence the workings of our minds through the operation of the laws of suggestion or association while we are awake; for it is impossible to hold in any intelligible fashion the doctrine of the agency of the Holy Spirit unless we make such an admission. But if God can thus influence our minds when we are awake, it is equally easy for Him to do so while we are asleep, so that there is no antecedent impossibility against the view that He may speak to men in and through the visions of the night.

Again, the providence of God must take cognizance of our dreams as well as of our waking thoughts, and must be equally in and over both, otherwise it is not really universal. Hence there is nothing either absurd or unphilosophical or impious in supposing that God may avail Himself of the phenomena of dreams for the purpose of turning the mind to His truth, or leading it into some particular direction. How He does that it is impossible to say. Sleep is a mystery, and dreams are a mystery, and to them both we may apply the words of Hamlet, " There are more things in heaven and earth than have been dreamed of in philosophy "; while, whatever may be said of dreams in general, we are probably not wrong in believing that the visions here recorded were from the Lord.

The chief butler and the chief baker, at least, had the conviction that their dreams were prophetic, and therefore we cannot wonder that when Joseph came to them in the morning he found them looking sad; and, acquainted as he was with sorrow in his own experience, it was quite natural for him to express his sympathy by asking, " Wherefore look ye so sadly to-day?" In response to his inquiry they said, " We have dreamed a dream, and there is no interpreter of it "; and he answered, " Do not interpretations belong to God? Tell me then, I pray you." Not that he claimed to be God, but that he had within him the consciousness that now his opportunity had come, and that God would enable him to take advantage of it by giving him the insight for the exposition of their visions. And we cannot but feel that in this faith of his we have the secret of Joseph's greatness. Many a man, having had his experience of dreams, would have said to these prisoners, " Think no more about them; they are mere delusions. I too have had my dreams; and once they seemed to me prophetic, but they have only mocked me, and it will be the same with you." But no, he was holding himself up by his faith in God's revelation to himself, made long ago through the bowing sheaves and the reverential stars, and he would not make light of what had been similarly revealed to other men.

With far-reaching suggestiveness, a thoughtful preacher has said,* " Joseph's willingness to interpret the dreams of his fellow-prisoners proves that he still believed in his own; that among his other qualities he had this characteristic also of a steadfast and profound soul, that he 'reverenced as a man the dreams of his youth.' Had he not done so, and had he not yet hoped that somehow God would bring truth out of them, he would surely have said, 'Don't you believe in dreams; they will only get you into difficulties.' He would have said, what some of us could dictate from our own thoughts, 'I won't meddle with dreams any more; I am not so young as I once was; doctrines and principles that served for fervent romantic youth seem puerile now, when I have learned what human life actually is. I can't ask this man, who knows the world, and has held the cup for Pharaoh, and is aware what a practical shape the king's anger takes, to cherish hopes similar to those which often seem so remote and doubtful to myself. My religion has brought me into trouble; it has lost me my situation; it has kept me poor; it has made me despised; it has debarred me from enjoyment. Can I ask this man to trust to inward whisperings which have so misled me? No! no! let every man bear his own burden. If he wishes to become religious, let not me bear the responsibility; if he will dream, let him find some other interpreter.'" But not thus did he speak to the two heart-stricken

* Dr. Marcus Dod's "Isaac, Jacob, and Joseph," pp. 180, 181.

captives; and in offering to become the interpreter of
their dreams he takes another step towards the fulfilment
of his own. Had he ridiculed their visions, then, so far as
we can see, he might have remained in the prison till
his death; but by the course he took, inspired as that
was by faith in God, he showed that he still regarded
his own visions as full of Divine significance, and took
the way that led to their verification.

When they heard his words of sympathy, the dreamers
told him their visions. We need not go into them in detail,
save to show how the dream of each rooted itself in and
grew out of his former occupation, and how they are
illustrated in almost every particular by the representations
found in these later years on the Egyptian monuments.
Thus Wilkinson tells us that the tombs at the Pyramids
show us pictures delineating grapes in the process of being
picked from the vines and put into baskets, and letting
us see the preparation of the grape-juice, from its being
pressed out of the clusters to its being stored in jars.
That fermented wine was drunk is evident from the
paintings of feasts, as also from the condition of the
women, to the representation of whom I have already
referred; while, that I may not seem to be ungallant,
it must be added that portraitures of men in a state of
helpless intoxication are not unknown. The kings, however, who were under the special regulation of the priests,
had their allowance fixed, and the kind of wine they were
to drink prescribed; and the representation in the dream
is literally in accord with a text "discovered by Ebers
in the inscriptions of the Temple of the Edfu, in which
the king is seen standing, cup in hand, while underneath
are the words, 'They press grapes into the water and the
king drinks.'"*

---

* Geikie's "Hours with the Bible," vol. i. p. 465.

In the dream of the chief baker we have similar resemblances to what we find on the monuments. Even so trifling a detail as the baked meats being said to be carried on the head is true to Egyptian life; for while men generally carried their burdens less often on their heads than otherwise, bakers were a marked exception, and there are actual instances in which confectioners are portrayed with baskets on their heads. A papyrus of the age when the Hebrews were in Egypt names four of Pharaoh's bakers, of whom one is always called 'the chief,' and the importance of his office may be judged from the fact that no fewer than 114,064 loaves are said to have been delivered by him at a particular time to the royal store-rooms." *

The dream of the cup-bearer was interpreted by Joseph to mean that within three days he would be restored to his office; and, showing the implicitness of his faith in the truth of the revelation, he accompanied his explanation with this pathetic statement and wistful request—" But think on me when it shall be well with thee, and shew kindness, I pray thee, unto me, and make mention of me unto Pharaoh, and bring me out of this house; for indeed I was stolen away out of the land of the Hebrews, and here also have I done nothing that they should put me into the dungeon." Ah! yes, captivity is still captivity, though the slave be set over other slaves; a prison is still a prison, though the prisoner be intrusted in it with the charge of others; and this plaintive appeal lets us see deep down in Joseph's heart to the very quick of his distress.

The dream of the chief cook, to his great disappointment—for his expectations were raised by the good things foretold to his companion—was explained by Joseph to

---

* Geikie, *ubi supra*, vol. i. p. 467.

mean "that in three days he should be hanged upon a
tree, and his body left to be eaten by the birds." And
both proved to be prophetic ; for the third day was
Pharaoh's birthday, and that was always celebrated among
the Egyptians with great festivity. Thus we learn from
Geikie that " an inscription of the time of the Exodus
tells us of Rameses II. that his birthday caused joy in
heaven. The priests of every class assembled in the
temples, an amnesty was granted to prisoners, and a great
feast was held worthy of a monarch who was worshipped
by his subjects. Under colour of recalling the glories of
the past year, the priesthood took the opportunity of re-
newing their hold on him by flattering but significant
addresses ; after which, surrounded by all his court and
the dignitaries of the temples, he .dispensed his grace or
favours as he thought fit."*

The punishment dealt out to the chief baker was very
severe. He was first beheaded, and then his body was
gibbeted upon a pole and left to be devoured by the birds.
The terror of this to an Egyptian was tremendous ; for in
his belief, as, indeed, is manifest from the embalming of
the dead, the preservation of the body was essential to
continued existence after death, and the leaving of it to be
destroyed was, therefore, fatal to all hopes of a happy
eternity. As Geikie says, " Beheading, preceded by beating with sticks, was a common punishment, but refusal of
embalmment was only pronounced against extraordinary
offenders. To leave the body to be eaten by the dogs was
the most terrible item in the punishment of the treacherous
wife in the ' Tale of the Two Brothers.' " †

So the two men passed out on the third morning from
the prison, one to the palace and the other to the gibbet,
and Joseph remained behind, waiting in the heart-sickness

---

* Geikie's " Hours with the Bible," vol. i. p. 468.
† Geikie, *ibid*, p. 487.

of " hope deferred " for some result from the intercession
of the chief cup-bearer with Pharaoh on his behalf. But
alas for the ingratitude of men ! the chapter ends with
these doleful words, " Yet did not the chief butler remember Joseph but forgat him."

Now in seeking to turn the incidents of this portion of
the narrative to profitable account, we find some important
truths suggested for our consideration.

We cannot but be struck with the minute particularity
of the Providence of God. Indeed, this is the one great
truth which, as we shall see, runs like a thread through
the whole of this history, and on which all its incidents
are strung; so that we might use Joseph's own words as a
motto for it all—" Ye thought evil against me, but God
meant it unto good."   Think of the coincidence which
brought the Ishmaelites to the spot at which his brothers
were feasting at the very moment when he was in the pit
hard by.   Think, again, of his being bought, of all people
in Egypt, by Potiphar, the captain of the guard, and of
his being cast into the prison, for no fault of his own, but
on a false accusation, and of his being still there at the
very time when these two high officials of the court were
consigned by Pharaoh to the same place of confinement.
Behold at how many critical points his life touches the
lives of others, and is, thereby, carried so much the farther
forward towards the attainment by him of the place which
God was preparing for him. Suppose we found these
things in a novel, we should say that they were all
designed by its author for the development and unravel-
ment of what he calls his plot. Very well. But is there
no plot in a human life ? How else shall we account for
the appearance of a plot in fiction—which is meant to be
a delineation of life—and which, wherever it is a work of
true genius, is a delineation of life, if there be not in every
human life that which corresponds to a plot ? Is it not

true, as Dr. Bushnell has said in one of his wonderful sermons, that " every man's life is a plan of God " ? and if one were to say to you that such coincidences are only found in novels, could you not say to him, " It is not so, for I have met them in my own career " ? I know, at least, that I have had as wonderful things in that way in my own experience as I ever read of in fiction; and if in the fiction I must trace them to the plan of the author, why must I be debarred in real life from tracing them to the plan of God ? When I get to a great railway junction, and find trains coming in together from the east, and the north, and the south, just in time to join another that is starting from that point for the west, I should be regarded as a simpleton if I spoke of that as a wonderful coincidence. And yet, on the great Railroad of Life, when I come to such a junction, and meet there a train that leads me on to some significant sphere of service, I am supposed to be a simpleton if I refer that to the overruling Providence of God. But I am not a simpleton—I am only reasoning in that department as I would in the domain of literature or daily travelling; and he who repudiates God's Providence is the fool, according to that scathing utterance of the Psalmist — " The *fool* hath said in his heart there is no God."

But we are reminded by this history also that the character of the individual has as much to do with what I have called the development of the plot of his life as the plan or purpose of God has. Providence is not fatalism. Joseph, if he had chosen to act otherwise than he did, might have thrown away all the opportunities which these places of junction in his life afforded him. If he had stormed against his brothers with violent resistance they might have been provoked to slay him out of hand; but his demeanour of patience and meekness moved Reuben to seek to save his life. If, again, in the house of Potiphar he had been, as we phrase it, "ugly" and ill-tempered, determined, because he was a slave, and unjustly deprived of his liberty, that he would make everybody uncomfortable around him, he would never have risen to any honour or eminence in his master's house, but would have been set to do the lowest and most degrading menial work.   If, again, when his temptation came to him, he had sinfully yielded, he never would have been consigned to the prison, and would have had no opportunity of serving the cup-bearer. Nay, if he had not made himself useful and agreeable in the prison, he would have had no chance of rendering the service which is here recorded—a service which, as Joseph himself seemed to feel, and which, as we know from the subsequent history, had so much to do with his ultimate elevation to the second place in the kingdom.   Thus, the character of Joseph was here a co-worker with the Providence of God.   He fell in with God's plan.   He had educated himself so that he could see the chance—speaking after the manner of men—when it came, and could use it to the highest advantage.   And by all this he was steadily preparing himself for the place which God in His plan was preparing for him.   Again then, I say, Providence is not fatalism, and if you would avail yourself of the opportunities which God furnishes you at the critical turnings of your history, you must watch your character, and seek so to meet everything as from Him, and so to serve Him in everything, that when the important time arrives you can recognise its value, and improve it for His glory in your own advancement.   The men that fail in life do not fail for want of such opportunities as Joseph had, but for want of the character to see these opportunities, and the ability to use them.   Keep near to God, therefore, form your character according to His principles, and then, even though you may be in a prison, you will find a way to serve Him, and will feel that somehow you are

on the road to your success, and in training for your
sphere.

But we may learn that those who have been themselves
upheld in trouble are the most efficient helpers of others
when they are in trial. Young as Joseph was, he had seen
enough of sorrow to dispose him to sympathise with others
in their affliction. And in the suggestive question which
he put to his fellow-prisoners, "Do not interpretations
belong to God?" he not only expresses his own faith, but
in the most delicate and skilful manner indicates to them
the source whence alone true consolation comes. His
faith in God had been grievously tried. He had been
plunged into affliction, and as the direct and immediate
result of his adherence to the course of purity and rectitude, he had been cast into a prison. Yet he still held fast
his confidence in Jehovah, and it was that faith which
made him such a cheerful comforter of others. There was
a great sorrow in his heart, but his firm conviction that
God was ordering his life made him outwardly happy in
spite of that; and only on such an occasion as that of his
appeal to the cup-bearer was any reference made to it
by him. But the consciousness that it was there opened
his ear in compassion for the reception of the story of
another's woe. Yes, it is only through suffering that
we learn to sympathise, and that, I think, is what
the sacred writer specially refers to when he says
even of Christ that " He was made perfect through
suffering." " The Lord God gave Him the tongue of
the learned that He might know to speak a word in season
to him that is weary." But He gave it to Him not as a
ready-made endowment. He gave it to Him through days
of exhaustive manual labour at Nazareth; through privations as He went over Palestine with nowhere to lay His
head; through Satanic temptations in the wilderness;
through the bitter ingratitude and malicious attacks of men;

through the agony of the garden and the ignominy of the Cross—so that it could be said regarding Him, "In that He Himself hath suffered being tempted, or tried, He is able to succour them that are tried." And it is with the disciples as it was with the Master. The greatest sufferers among them are those best qualified to sympathise.

More than thirty years ago, just at the beginning of my ministry, I was in the house of a beloved pastor when he was called to pass through the greatest trial that a man can know, in the death of a truly good and noble wife. Two mornings after, the postman brought in a sheaf of letters. I think there were more than twenty of them, but each was from a brother minister who *had been led through the same dark valley*, and who was seeking to comfort him with the comfort wherewith he himself had been comforted of God. Only a few evenings ago I met a Christian lady, with whom I was comparing notes regarding the experience of the loss of little children, and she said to me, " I never see the death of a little child announced in the newspaper but I have an impulse to write to the parents and speak comfortably to them." Thus we may console ourselves under our own trials with the thought that God is endowing us thereby with the gift of sympathy, and fitting us to become " sons of consolation " to others in affliction. You wonder, perhaps, at the tenderness of sympathy which some friend evinces ; you are astonished how he should know to speak just the right things to you in your trial, but if you were familiar with his history you would cease to be surprised, for he is only repeating to you what God wrote upon his own heart in the day when he was himself in trouble.

But that thought reminds me to add that mere suffering will not give us the gift of consolation, unless we have ourselves been sustained by God through our affliction. We can say, then, that the anchor which held us in the storm will hold others, and that saying has more staying power in it than if we were merely to direct the troubled one to use an anchor which we had never proved. When you are in the prison, therefore, remember that you are there not simply for your own sake, to prepare you for the post that you are yet to fill, but for the sake of others, that you may learn to speak a word in season to those who shall be in it after you. In the Tower of London the walls of some of its chambers are all written over with inscriptions made by prisoners, and some of these are of the most touching character, such as I doubt not gave much comfort to those who read them just before their own execution. And so it seems to me that in our trials God leads us through experiences which shall enable us, by their mere rehearsal, to uphold others when they come to be in like circumstances. The price is costly, but the learning is precious.

Finally, we are reminded that those whom we benefit have often very poor remembrance of our kindness. Men too often write the record of grudges in marble and of favours in water. If one has done us an injury we do not easily forget that, but if we have received a benefit we let the remembrance of that slip out of our minds. Nay, such is the perversity of human nature, that not unfrequently men return evil for the good which has been done them. One spoke to an English statesman of the violent enmity which another evinced towards him. "Yes," was the reply, "and I cannot understand it, for I never did him any kindness that I can remember." The sarcasm was bitter, but there was enough of truth in it to give it point ; and every one who seeks to be a helper of others learns, sooner or later, to give over looking for human gratitude, and to think mainly of the Lord Jesus Christ and His appreciation. If you tread upon a tender toe you will be sure to hear of that ; but if you have been

helpful to another, if you have been the means of giving
him hope and joy and inspiration, if you have lifted him
out of the slough of despondency and sent him on his way,
you may never know anything about that until it be
revealed to you at last by the Lord. Ah! this chief
butler has had too many like him in all ages. The return
of prosperity makes men forget the benefactors of their
adversity. What then? Why should we whimper over
that?—the more especially as there is One, and He the
Best and Highest of all, who stands out in striking
contrast to all such as this cup-bearer represents.
Elevation has changed many a man's heart and turned
many a man's head. But " Jesus Christ is the same
yesterday, to-day, and forever"; the same on the throne
of glory that He was on earth eighteen hundred years ago.
He will remember us, and whatsoever we do for Him in
the service of our fellow-men, however they may forget it,
will be acknowledged by Him. He remembers us now, for
He is making intercession for us; and He will recognise us
at the last, for " the cup of cold water given to a disciple
in the name of a disciple shall in no wise lose its reward."
What matters human ingratitude, then, when we have
Divine recognition? Endure the prison a little longer.
The chariot and the throne will be here erelong.

VI.

PROMOTION AT LAST.

GENESIS xli. 14-6.

FOR two full years after the restoration of the cup-
bearer to his office Joseph remained in the prison,
occupying the position to which, for his trustworthiness
and integrity, he had been raised. But although this
delay was due to the ungrateful forgetfulness of the man
to whom he had shown so much kindness, and for whose
intercession with the monarch he had so touchingly made
request; and although that official was really blameworthy
for his neglect; yet the overruling Providence of God is
clearly seen, both in the occasion on which and the time
at which Joseph's services were recalled to the remembrance of the butler, and brought by him to the notice
of the king. For if immediately after his own release,
and apart from the prospect of Joseph's being able to
render his majesty a service, in a time of great anxiety,
which no one else could perform, the cup-bearer had
reported Joseph's case to the king, it does not seem
that Pharaoh would have done more for him than transfer
him to some other department in which he would have
been still a slave, or at the most given him liberty to
return to Canaan, to his father's house and the persecution of his brothers, and in either case he would have
gone forth to obscurity. As it was, however, when the
door of the prison opened for him he went straight out
to that opportunity by the improvement of which he rose

at once to the second place in the greatest kingdom which
was then upon the earth.   Thus, through the apparently
long delay, he got all the sooner to his destination in the
end ; and that which seemed to hold him back a dreary
while from his promotion really expedited his elevation.
Now, in all this we have a lesson which is especially
valuable to you, young men.   You may be conscious
that you have it in you to do great things in the world.
You also may have had your dreams of rising to some
post of honour and usefulness in the city or in the land,
and you may have the assurance that these are prophetic
of what you are yet to become.   But just at present you
may be in a position in which it is impossible for you
to take any steps for your advancement.   You, too, have
been disappointed in finding that those whom you have
served, and on whose influence you had counted for the
securing of something nobler, have entirely forgotten you.
You are longing for an opportunity to better yourself,
but there is no apparent outlet for you.   Without being
immured in a dungeon, you are yet virtually in a prison ;
for you are hemmed in by circumstances, and chained by
limitations.   You are as high as you can ever reach where
you are, and you cannot change your place.   What then ?
Learn from Joseph here to bide your time, or, rather, to
wait God's time.   Serve Him a little longer where you
are, and by-and-bye He will set before you " an open door "
which no man can shut, and through which you will pass
at once to the place which is emphatically and peculiarly
your own.   Your strength meanwhile, therefore, is to sit
still.   Be patient until it is God's time for you to rise,
and when that comes no power will be able to hold you
down.   As the Prayer-book version of the old Psalm has
it, " Tarry the Lord's leisure."   Make haste slowly.   Do
the duties of your present sphere.   Remember that " all
things come to the feet of him who waits," provided only

he works and prays while he waits. Ambition pants for greatness; but piety sanctifies ambition, so that it is content to wait until it can rise in God's time and by God's way.

Nor must we lose sight of the fact that by those years of prison life, as well as by the temptation and privations by which they were preceded, Joseph's character was steadied into strength and ripened into maturity, so that when his opportunity came he used it with splendid effect. They did for him what his forty years in Midian did for Moses, and his eighteen months in Arabia did for Paul. They threw him in upon himself, and back upon God. They disciplined him into calm self-possession, because they gave him a strong hold upon Jehovah. The forgetfulness of men led him to rely all the more implicitly on the memory of God. It might be a trial to him—it no doubt was at first—to see the man whose dream he had interpreted go out at once to its fulfilment, while he had waited many long years for the realisation of his own, and seemed as far from it as ever.

But however much he might yield to such feelings for a time, the sequel proves that he had ultimately risen above them. Abraham had to wait long for Isaac; Isaac had to wait long for the birth of his sons; Jacob had to spend twenty years in Padan-aram before the coming of that Peniel night which secured him in the covenant inheritance. What was he better than they that he should have an immediate fulfilment of the promise made to him? So his knowledge of the experience of his ancestors came now to his assistance, and long before Isaiah's day he found out for himself Isaiah's principle, " He that believeth shall not make haste." Many a man in his circumstances would have become cynical and misanthropic, saying, " To what purpose do I serve others if they so forget my service?" but his suffering sent him to Jehovah, and in fellowship with Him he not only retained that disposition to help others, which was so distinct a feature of his earlier days, but also acquired that calm, resolute equipoise of spirit which he so conspicuously manifested in his later life. They say that the palm-tree grows stronger the heavier the weight that is put upon it ; so, when a man cleaves to God, difficulty only disciplines him into greatness, and imprisonment only teaches him how to make the best of his liberty.

Remark, too, that all this was the result of God's overruling the sinful forgetfulness of man. Many would limit God's Providence to things which come directly from His hand. Only the other day a sufferer, to my surprise, declined my offer to pray with him, because his suffering, as he said, was the result of a human blunder, and was to be got rid of simply by rectifying that. But here God's Providence both overruled a human sin and brought good out of it ; and the Lord is always working yet in the same way. I have heard, too, of one reproving a servant after this fashion : " If it were a dispensation of Providence, I could bear it ; but I can have no patience with your stupidity "—as if there had been no Providence in his having such a servant, and there were no duty devolving on him in consequence. But all such views are reproved by the history before us, in which we see that in some inscrutable but real way God brings good out of evil, and makes even the mistakes and sins of men to work out His will in the disciplining and elevating of His people. Ah ! it is a wonderful thing, this Providence of God, and if we only fully believed in it we should know a little more of what Paul means when he speaks of " the peace of God that passeth all understanding " keeping our hearts and minds.

But now came the time for the revelation of Joseph's greatness. Nothing unusual seemed to herald its approach,.

and, for all that appears to the contrary, Joseph was taken unawares. But that only made the test of his character the more searching, for it showed him as he really was, and he did not suffer from the manifestation. All the officials about the household of the captain of the guard might be excited by the hasty appearance of messengers from Pharaoh. There might be a flutter among the prisoners, as each one thought that the summons might be for him, and knew not whether it might mean that he should be restored to liberty or be put to death. But Joseph was all himself; and though "the king's business required haste," he took time to prepare himself by observing the proprieties which he knew to be required of all who went in before the monarch. They were little things, and it might have been supposed that in the circumstances Pharaoh would have overlooked any breach of etiquette concerning them; but Joseph did not neglect them, and by his attention to them he showed his real greatness. For while it is the mark of a small mind to give its entire thought to such matters, it is by no means an indication of superior intelligence to ignore them altogether; and few incidents in this entire history give us such a clear insight into the wisdom and self-possession, or what we may call presence of mind of Joseph, as the little thing here recorded regarding him—that " he shaved himself and changed his raiment " before he went into the presence of the king. In regard to this matter of the toilet, the better classes of Egyptians were exceedingly punctilious. I quote the following sentences from Wilkinson[*] in illustration : " ' The Egyptians,' says Herodotus, ' only let the hair of their head and beard grow in mourning, being at all other times shaved ' ; which agrees perfectly with the authority of the Bible, and of the

---

[*] " Ancient Egyptians," vol. ii. pp. 330, 331.

sculptures.   So particular, indeed, were they on this
point, that to have neglected it was a subject of reproach
and ridicule ; and whenever they intended to convey the
idea of a man of low condition, or a slovenly person, the
artists represented him with a beard.   It is amusing to
find that their love of caricature was not confined to the
lower orders, but extended even to the king ; and the
negligent habits of Rameses VII. are indicated on his
tomb at Thebes by the appearance of his chin, blackened
by an unshorn beard of two or three days' growth.   The
same habits of cleanliness are also indicated by the
changes of raiment given by Joseph to his brethren when
they set out to bring their father to Egypt."   By his
attention to these matters, therefore, Joseph proved
himself to be, in the true sense of the word, a "gentle-
man," who was willing in all minor things to conform
to the usages of the society into which he was about
to enter.

But while he is thus preparing himself for standing
before Pharaoh, we may take the opportunity of explaining
why he came to be sent for in such haste.   The case was
this: The king in the same night had dreamed two dreams
of such a peculiar sort that they filled his mind with
anxiety as to the prosperity of the land over which he was
the ruler.   And any one in the least degree acquainted
with the symbolism and sentiments of the ancient Egyptians
will understand at once how he came to be so much excited by his visions.   In the first he saw seven kine
coming up out of the Nile in splendid condition, and
feeding on the soft, succulent grass which grew in abun-
dance on the margin of the river ; but after them came up
other seven lean and ill-favoured kine, which actually ate
up the others.   In the second he saw seven ears of corn,
large and good, which again were devoured by seven thin
and blasted ears.   Now here was the river which was

recognised by them all as the great source of the fertility
of the country; here were cows which, in the mythology
of the people, were the symbols of the productive power
of the earth; here also were ears of corn, themselves the
fruits of that productive power; evidently, therefore, the
dreams were such as not only concerned the welfare of
the country, but were also intimately related to each other;
while the similar feature in each of them, that the one of
the two groups of animals and ears was devoured by the
other, might not obscurely indicate that they both referred
to one and the same thing. Indeed, as with Joseph's
interpretation of them before us we now read the account
of these visions, we rather wonder that the magicians and
the wise men should have been baffled by what seems to
us so plain. But it is only another illustration of the
truth so humorously enforced in the well known story of
Columbus and the egg. It is easy to open a lock when
you have found the key, but to find the key, or to make it,
is the difficulty; and by that difficulty, in this case, the
learned men of the court were overcome. They could not
tell the king the meaning of his visions.

Naturally, that would only make his anxiety the greater;
and every one who came into personal contact with him
would be as troubled as he was himself. So the chief
butler came to know of his perplexity, and immediately
the similarity of the case to that of the chief baker and
himself in the prison recalled Joseph to his thoughts, so
that he was moved to tell the king of his experience. The
manner in which that was done by him is exceedingly
adroit. He treads very lightly over the fact of his having
been in prison at all, and he finishes his story without
making any suggestion, leaving Pharaoh to draw his own
inference and come to his own determination. But the
effect was precisely that which he had anticipated, for the
king sent at once for Joseph; and the haste with which his

servants acted on his commission is but an incidental corroboration of the fact that he was eagerly impatient for
the appearance of the man of whom he had just heard
such a wonderful story.

Behold, then, Joseph before the king! He has just
touched his thirtieth year, and the alertness of youth is still
in his eyes and in his frame, but over his face there is "the
pale cast of thought," and on his brow the development of
a maturity beyond his age. Thirteen years have gone
since that day when, in his gay apparel, he left his
father's tent at Hebron, little more than a boy; but each of
these cycles has left its own deposit of experience on his
character, and given him a better knowledge at once of his
God and of himself, so that he stands now unabashed
before the majesty of Egypt. Pharaoh states the case to
him, and says, "I have heard say of thee that thou canst
understand a dream to interpret it," and he at once
replied, "It is not in me; God shall give Pharaoh an
answer of peace." He would have no honour that did
not belong to him, and he has one message both to the
servants and the master. To them he had said—and that
part of the conversation the chief butler had forgotten to
report—"Do not interpretations belong to God?" and
to him he answers, "It is not in me; God shall give
Pharaoh an answer of peace." On the one hand, humility; on the other, faith. These two should always go
together, and the union of the two secures the co-operation
of Jehovah.

After hearing the dreams, Joseph read at once the
meaning of the symbols, and declared that the country
was about to enjoy seven good years, during which the
land would yield unusually abundant crops, but that
they would be followed by seven consecutive years of
exceptional scarcity, amounting even, as they advanced,
to actual famine, during which the superabundance of

the preceding time of plenty would be entirely consumed.
He added that the doubling of the dream was "because
the thing was established by God, and God would shortly
bring it to pass." Then showing how thoroughly he
believed in the truth of his own interpretation—which,
indeed, must have at once commended itself to the
acceptance of all who heard it—he went on to advise
that Pharaoh should immediately take measures to provide
against the danger of which he had been thus super-
naturally warned. He suggested that the land should
be divided into districts, and that over each of these a
trusty officer should be placed, who should receive the fifth
part of each year's produce, which was the government's
portion, and should store that up in granaries in the cities
against the coming time of famine.

There was so much practical wisdom evinced in the
suggestion, and so much executive ability manifested
in the manner in which it was proposed to carry it out,
that Pharaoh came to the conclusion that no time was
fitter for action than the present, and no man better
qualified to superintend the whole business than Joseph
himself. There and then, therefore, he raised Joseph
to the second place in the kingdom, invested him with
insignia appropriate to the office to which he had
appointed him, made him ride in the second chariot
which he had, sent him to make a formal tour of inspection
over all the land, and caused everywhere a proclamation
to be made before him to the effect that he should "rejoice
greatly," or that he was a "pure prince": for there is
some difference of opinion as to the meaning of the
Egyptian word here wrongly translated "Bow the knee";
and while some would make it signify "rejoice thou,"
others would interpret it as "pure prince."

To complete his exaltation, he was entered into the
caste of the priests, and received in marriage Asenath,

the daughter of Potiphera, the priest of the great Temple
of the Sun at On in Heliopolis, a city which stood on
the eastern bank of the Nile, a few miles from Memphis,
where there still exists an obelisk of red granite, with
a dedication sculptured by a monarch belonging to the
twelfth dynasty, which must, therefore, have been seen
by Joseph on the occasion of his marriage, and by Moses
when, as a student at the great seminary there, he was
educated in all the wisdom and learning of the Egyptians.

Besides these marks of honour, Joseph received a new
name from the king—analagous to those which Daniel
and his friends received, in a later age, from Nebuchadnezzar, and having some special appropriateness to the
work which he was to perform. Different explanations
have been given of its meaning. Some, like those who
drew up the marginal readings of our Bible, understand
by it " a revealer of secrets," but others, viewing the term
as really an Egyptian word in Hebrew letters, have put
it back again into its Egyptian form, getting, according to
Brugsch, the meaning, " the governor of the abode of
him who lives"; or, according to Canon Cooke, whose
dissertation in the " Speakers' Commentary" on the
Egyptian words in the Pentateuch is of very great value,
" the food of life," or " the food of the living." I am, of
course, imcompetent to judge between these scholars, but
I wish you to note, as a mark of the age of this history,
that we have here embedded in the Hebrew text Egyptian
words in Hebrew letters, to which, in this late day, our
Egyptologists, who have learned the language from the
inscriptions on the monuments, are able to give very
definite and intelligible translations—a fact which scarcely
comports with the notion, now so popular with some, that
this book is only a production of a very late date, composed, perhaps, 800 years after the events. But similar
conformation of the age of this record may be found in

the description of Joseph's investiture with office as compared with the representation of such ceremonies found upon the monuments. The history before us says, "And Pharaoh took off his ring from his hand and put it upon Joseph's hand, and arrayed him in vestures of fine linen, and put a gold chain about his neck." Now hear what Wilkinson tells us of the testimony of the monuments: "The investiture of a chief was a ceremony of considerable importance, when the post conferred was connected with any high dignity about the person of the monarch, in the army or the priesthood. It took place in the presence of the sovereign seated on his throne; and two priests having arrayed the candidate in a long, loose vesture, placed necklaces around the neck of the person thus honoured by the royal favour. One of these ceremonies frequently occurs in the monuments, which was sometimes performed immediately after a victory; in which case we may conclude that the honour was granted in return for distinguished services in the field; and as the individual on all occasions holds the flabella, crook, and other insignia of the office of fan-bearer, it appears to have been either the appointment to that post or to some high command in the army. On receiving this honourable distinction he held forth his hands in token of respect, and raising the emblems of his newly acquired office above his head, he expressed his fidelity to his king, and his desire to prove himself worthy of the favour he had received. A similar mode of investiture appears to have been adopted in all appointments to the high offices of state, both of a civil and military kind. In this, as in many customs detailed in the sculptures, we find an interesting illustration of a ceremony mentioned in the Bible, which describes Pharaoh taking a ring from his hand and putting it on Joseph's hand, arraying him in vestures of fine linen, and putting a gold chain about his neck." * And in another place† he says, " The immense difference of rank between the king and the highest nobles of the land is shown by their all walking on foot in attendance on the chariot of the king. And part of the great honour conferred on Joseph was his being placed in the second chariot that the king had ; giving him, in fact, the attendance of a king, as no one had a chariot or car while attending on a king."

Two difficulties are apt to strike the common reader. He is prone to consider it either unnatural or improbable that Joseph should be thus suddenly elevated, and that he should consent in this matter-of-course way to marry a wife who had been selected for him by the monarch. But as to the first of these, it may be said that cases of unexpected elevation are by no means uncommon in the East. We have other Scriptural illustrations of the same thing in the biographies of Daniel and Mordecai ; and even recent history is not without what may almost be called romantic instances of a similar sort. Thus Jamieson tells us‡ that in 1852 the Prime-minister of Persia " was the son of a donkey-driver, who rose, by the strength and energy of his character, to be the second man in rank, but really the first in power." Then as to the marriage, Bishop Browne is right when he says§ that " neither the Egyptians nor the Hebrews were at this time as exclusive as they became afterwards "; and we may add that we must not judge the conduct of Joseph in a case like this by the principles of the New Testament as now understood ; though, putting even the lowest construction on Joseph's conduct in the matter, it would not be difficult to find

---

* Wilkinson's " Ancient Egyptians," vol. iii. pp. 370, 371.
† *Ibid*, vol. i. p. 160.
‡ " Critical and Experimental Commentary," vol. i. p. 244.
§ " Speakers' Commentary," *in loco*.

many parallels to it in this age of boasted enlightenment, and this land of Bibles and churches.

But now, leaving mere exposition, let me turn your thoughts for a few moments to matters of personal concernment. I have left one subject comparatively untouched, and that is the secret of Joseph's elevation. Let me say, then, that the way of preferment is never permanently closed against any man. If one does not—as the phrase is—get on in life, it is not his circumstances but himself that is to blame. Occasionally, indeed, there may come reverses of fortune for which he cannot be held responsible, but the man who is always out at elbows and unfortunate must have something amiss in himself. Either he has not fitted himself to take advantage of his opportunities, or there is a leak somewhere in his character, through which his energies and abilities are drained off into useless or expensive directions.

In the England of to-day, and especially in the United States, no man needs be forever a hewer of wood or a drawer of water; and though sudden elevations like this of Joseph are not common in these days, yet there are men continually appearing among us who have come up from an obscurity as great as Joseph's to a position just as exalted as that which he ultimately reached. Both of the martyr-Presidents may be referred to as cases in point. Let young men, therefore, be encouraged. Do not sink into despair; do not imagine that the world is in league against you; but " learn to labour and to wait."

Two things especially you ought to bear in mind: first, that the true way to rise to a higher position is to fill well the lower which you already occupy. To borrow here from Thomas Binney, " Remember that to do as well as ever you can what happens to be the only thing within your power to do, is the best and surest preparation for higher service. Should things go against you, never give way to debilitating depression, but be hopeful, brave, courageous, careful not to waste in vain and unavailing regret the power you will need for endurance and endeavour. Learn well your business, whatever it be; make the best of every opportunity for acquiring any sort of knowledge that may enlarge your acquaintance with the business in general, and enable you to take advantage of any offer or opening that may come."* Then, again, take note that piety is no hindrance to the right sort of success. Joseph did not hide his allegiance to God or his faith in God, and these even commended him to Pharaoh. So there are many heads of great establishments or corporations in the world who, though they care nothing for religion themselves, would prefer that their trusted servants should be godly men. Sometimes, no doubt, inflexible adherence to the right and the true may cost a man his place, even as here resistance to temptation sent Joseph for a while to prison; but in the end I do not think that any man ever lost by his religion, provided his religion was the real thing, and not a make-believe. It may lengthen the road a little; it may add to the difficulties of the journey; it may take him through some very dark passages, but it will lead him generally at last to honour and influence; for "godliness *is* profitable unto all things, having the promise of the life that now is and of that which is to come."

But there is a success higher and better than that of outward position and wealth, and even when riches are not gained that is always attainable. You cannot all become millionaires, or merchant princes, or political leaders, or governors of States, or presidents of the United States—that is an impossibility; but you can all be good and noble men, if you will. As I have often said, good character is the true success of life, and "that

---

* " From Seventeen to Thirty," p. 86.

character is the best which is real and thorough—true and genuine to the core—which has nothing underlying it of the consciousness of secret sin, which is as pure and unspotted as it is thought to be, and the moral and manly virtues of which are based upon, and inspired by, religious faith, by that love and fear of God which at once preserve from 'great transgressions' and prompt to the cultivation of every personal and social virtue."* Get a character like that. To that end begin by laying as its foundation-stone faith in Jesus Christ; then go on, according to Peter's plan, by adding " to your faith courage, and to courage knowledge, and to knowledge temperance, and to temperance patience, and to patience godliness, and to godliness brotherly kindness, and to brotherly kindness love; for if ye do these things ye shall never fall, for so an entrance shall be ministered unto you abundantly into the everlasting kingdom of our Lord and Saviour Jesus Christ." Such an entrance is life's true success, and that is attainable by every one of you if you choose to work for it in the way that the Apostle prescribes.

---

* Binney's " From Seventeen to Thirty," p. 87.

VII.

PUBLIC ADMINISTRATION.

GENESIS xli. 47-52 ; xlvii. 13-26.

DURING the seven years of plenty, which began with the elevation of Joseph to the second position in the land of Egypt, there were born to him two sons, to whom he gave Hebrew names, from the significance of which we may learn something of the deepest feelings of his heart. He called the eldest Manasseh, which means "forgetting"; "for," said he, "God hath made me forget all my toil, and all my father's house." Not that he had ceased, or that he ever could cease, to look back with delight on the home at Hebron, where he had enjoyed so much of his father's affection, and had received those principles of religion and morality which he had so firmly held and so faithfully followed all through his life. Only the most slavish literalism, which loses sight of the real sentiment in its microscopic analysis of the words in which it is expressed, could bring any such meaning out of his language. It partakes of the hyperbolical character of the saying of our Lord, "If any man come to Me, and hate not his father and mother ... he cannot be My disciple"; * and it has its exact parallel in the words of the Psalm, which represents the suitor as saying to her whom he desires to make his spouse, "Hearken, O daughter, and consider, and incline thine ear ; forget also thine own people, and thy father's house." † Joseph was

---

* Luke xiv. 26. † Psalm xlv. 10.

very far indeed from having lost his interest in Jacob, or from seeking to cut himself off from the blessings of the covenant to whose birthright he had succeeded. That is made very clear in the subsequent history, not only by his inquiries after his father when his brothers came to buy food, and by his reception of the patriarch himself when he came to Egypt, but also by his dying request that when his descendants should leave that land on their return to Canaan they should carry thither with them his remains. What his words here imply, therefore, is that now, for the first time since he was sold to the Arabian traders, he had a home of his own, which was the earthly centre of his heart, and which ever attracted him back to its happiness from all his journeyings hither and thither in his official capacity. He was no more a mere unit in the vast population of a foreign land, but he had become the head of a household which gathered into it the holiest joys of his life, and the father of a son on whom he might lavish affection of a sort which his heart had not known in all his Egyptian experiences. Now, for the first time, he had found a home, and by that he was reconciled to his absence from his kindred.

To his second son he gave the name Ephraim, which signifies " fruitful"; for he said, " God hath caused me to be fruitful in the land of my affliction." If anything were needed to prove the correctness of the explanation which I have just offered of the meaning of Manasseh, it is the fact that here Joseph speaks of Egypt as " the land of his affliction," betokening that, with all its compensations, which went so far to reconcile him to his lot in it, that country was still to him a land of affliction; and that, like the patriarchs in Canaan, he was still looking for "a better country, that is, the heavenly." But most interesting of all it is to mark how he steadily recognises the hand of God in all the circumstances of his life. " *God* hath

made me to forget my toil." "*God* hath made me fruitful." This was the faith that kept him from despair when
he was in the pit and in the dungeon, and now it preserves
him from pride when, as the second ruler in the kingdom,
he is rejoicing over the little ones in his home. It sanc-
tified to him his prosperity as well as his adversity, and
allowed neither of them to hurt him. The triumph of the
horologist is seen in the construction of that compensation
balance which gives an equable movement to the chrono-
meter, undisturbed either by the cold of the arctic regions
or the heat of the torrid zone; and the power of faith in
God is manifested by the evenliness of disposition which
it enables the believer to maintain alike in trouble and in
joy. Nothing so strikes us in the character of Joseph all
through his history as what I may call the "stable
equilibrium" which he invariably preserved; and here we
see the foundation on which it rested—in his faith in God.

But while he is to be highly commended in that particular, it must, I think, be confessed that in his neglect
to communicate with his father, especially after his
elevation to his dignity, we have what appears to be a
serious fault in his conduct. For at least twenty-one
years he allowed Jacob to remain in utter ignorance of his
existence. Perhaps some excuse might be given for him
while he was a slave in the house of Potiphar, and it was
clearly impossible for him to convey any message to
Canaan when he was a prisoner. But after his exaltation
one would have expected that he would have attempted
in some way to open up communication with his father.
It may be said, indeed, that in those days there were no
such means of intercourse between distant places as we
now so fully enjoy; but still, for one in Joseph's high
position, we may be sure that if the will had been very
strong, the way would very easily have been found.
Others may suggest that the knowledge of all that had

been done to him might only have made matters worse between Jacob and his sons, and might have turned the brothers in exasperation against Benjamin; and that, because of the fear of these consequences, Joseph chose rather to keep silent and wait until God in His own way should bring about the fulfilment of the dream which promised that the father and the brothers together should do homage at his feet. And if any choose to rest in these explanations they may do so, but for my own part I cannot acquit Joseph here of unfilial conduct. To me it seems that so soon as he was a free man, and had the means at his disposal, he ought to have sent a messenger to tell his father that he was alive and well, and that God had raised him to an exalted position in the land of Egypt.

I cannot help pausing here for a moment to enforce upon young men residing in the great city and away from home the duty of maintaining a regular correspondence with their parents. Is it not too true that there are many who let long intervals elapse without writing home, and whose letters, when they do write, are of the most unsatisfactory sort, containing little or nothing but excuses for not having written sooner, and apologies for having so little to say. But, as Mr. Binney says, " the value of a letter from a young man in the city to the far-off town or village home consists in its little details—its affectionate gossip, its account of any circumstance or incident that may have promise in it of advantage, its story of hopeful struggle, of dawning success, or its references to new-formed friendships; to books read, churches attended, lectures listened to, with a thousand things besides, which may be small in themselves, but which show an interest in the home circle, and manifest the beating of ' the child's heart within the man's.' "* *You* are perhaps so occupied

---

* " From Seventeen to Thirty," p. 89.

day after day and week after week that you may have
little leisure to think of those in the old homestead.   In
the bustle of the workshop, or the store, or the counting-
room, many things force themselves upon your attention,
and you do not miss your relations.   But your parents,
having no such multiplicity of things to divert their minds,
are continually thinking about you; and as, morning after
morning, no letter comes from you, the effect is dis-
appointing and depressing.   They are apt to think that
you have forgotten them, and the neglect chills their
hearts.   Do not, I beseech you, let this occur with you;
and if you have been guilty of such thoughtlessness in the
past, take the earliest opportunity of repairing the evil;
yea, before you sleep to-night, sit down and write a hearty,
cheery letter to them, and tell them, if you like, how you
came to think of doing so; thereby you will warm their
spirits by the assurance of your continued love, and
benefit your own souls by the doing of a filial deed; for
thus it is written in the royal law, "Honour thy father
and thy mother, that thy days may be long upon the land
which the Lord thy God giveth thee."

And should there be some youth who has run away from
home, and left his parents in cruel ignorance as to whether
he is alive or dead, or, if alive, what his condition may be,
let me take this opportunity to urge such an one, whatever
the consequence may be, to send at once and let the sad
ones know where he is, and how it is with him.   Think of
it !   Since you left, every night on which the wind has
howled loud, or the rain has brattled noisily on the window-
panes, or the snow has fallen thick and blinding through
the darkness, these old people have said one to another,
"Where can that poor boy be in such a storm ?   God help
him !"   And you, in thoughtless indifference, are leaving
them in that dark suspense which is always worse than
the most terrible of certainties.   Shame on you for your

selfish and inconsiderate harshness to those whom you ought to love best in all the world! Go at once and telegraph to them that you are here, that they may with gladdened hearts be brought to say, " This our son was dead and is alive again, he was lost and is found."

But now, leaving Joseph's domestic history, let us examine his public administration. In order to get a complete view of that, it will be necessary to take into consideration certain particulars which are detailed * in a later section of the narrative, but it will be convenient to group them together here, and so to dispose of the matter once for all. As soon as he was appointed to his office, Joseph made a tour throughout the land, and had storehouses erected in all the cities. During the seven years of plenty, which came according to his prediction, the crops were exceedingly abundant; and of these he either took or bought for the king a fifth part, which he stored in the granaries—" the food of the field, which was round about every city, laid he up in the same." For a time a strict account was kept of all that was stored in each building, according to a fashion found illustrated quite frequently on the monuments; but at length the quantity became so great that they gave up trying to keep a formal register. This went on through the years of plenty. But when those of scarcity began, the face of things was changed; for the people, though apparently warned of what was coming, had not followed Joseph's example, and had made, of themselves, no preparation to meet the evil. The consequence was that they speedily exhausted all their available resources, and came to him for food. Here it is well to note that in the records of Egypt there is mention made of at least one other period of famine which lasted for seven years, and from the

---

* Chap. xlvii. 13, 26.

account of the sufferings which the people then endured,
we may have some little idea of the terrible privations
from which Joseph's contemporaries were saved through
his instrumentality. It occurred in the years A.D. 1064-
1071, and I take the following account of it from an article
in Smith's "Dictionary of the Bible": "Vehement drought
and pestilence continued for seven consecutive years, so
that the people ate corpses and animals that died of
themselves; the cattle perished; a dog was sold for five
deenars, and a cat for three deenars; and an ardebb
(about five bushels) of wheat for one hundred deenars,
and then it failed altogether." The author from whom
these details are taken (Es-Suyootee, in his Hosn el Mohá-
darah MS.) adds that "all the horses of the Khaleefeh
save three perished, and gives numerous instances of the
straits to which the wretched inhabitants were driven, and
of the organised bands of kidnappers who infested Cairo,
and caught passengers in the streets by ropes furnished
with hooks and let down from the houses. This account
is confirmed by El-Makreezee (in his Khitat), from which
we further learn that the family and even the women of
the Khaleefeh fled, by the way of Syria, on foot, to escape
the peril that threatened all ranks of the population." *
So again, Hengstenberg, quoting from Abdollatiph, has
the following concerning another Egyptian famine: "In
the year 1199 the height of the flood was small, almost
without example. The consequence was a terrible famine,
accompanied by indescribable enormities. Parents consumed their children; human flesh was, in fact, a very
common article of food; they contrived various ways of
preparing it. They spoke of it, and heard it spoken of,
as an indifferent affair. Man-eating became a regular
business. The greater part of the population was swept

---

* Smith's "Dictionary of the Bible," art. FAMINE.

away by death. In the following year, also, the inundation did not reach the proper height, and only the low lands were overflowed. Also much of that which was inundated could not be sown for want of labourers and seed-corn ; also of the seed which escaped this destruction a great part produced only meagre shoots, which perished." * These things might have been suffered in the case before us even to a more frightful extent, but for the policy that Joseph inaugurated and carried through ; and in judging that policy that fact ought to be taken into account. It is interesting also to know that the good work which he performed receives illustration, and perhaps corroboration, from the monuments and inscriptions. Thus, in the tombs of Beni Hassan, Ameni, a high officer of King Osirtasin I. of the twelfth dynasty, supposed to have been contemporary with Abraham, records this of himself : " For years I exercised my power as governor in the name of Mah. The hungry did not exist in my time, even when there were years of famine." And Brugsch tells us that on the tomb of Baba the following words are found : " I collected the harvest, a friend of the harvest god. I was watchful at the time of saving ; and now, when a famine arose, lasting many years, I issued out corn to the city at each famine." Nay, more, after having given some good arguments in support of his opinion, that eminent Egypto-logist affirms that " the only just conclusion is that the many years of famine in the time of Baba must precisely correspond with the seven years of famine under Joseph's Pharaoh, one of the Shepherd kings." †

But Joseph did not give the grain to the people for nothing. Such a practice carried on for seven years would only have demoralised them. So he sold it to them, first

---

* Quoted in " Joseph and his Times," by Thornley Smith, pp. 106, 107.
† Brugsch's " True Story of the Exodus of Israel," &c., pp. 131-2.

for their money ; then, when that was exhausted, for their
cattle ; then, when their cattle had been all transferred
into the royal hands, he, at their own suggestion, and in
accordance with their own urgent request, bought their
lands. Thus, from being peasant proprietors of the soil
they became tenants in fee to the government, and bound
themselves to pay as a rental the fifth part of the increase
of their fields year by year continually. It is even said
that he bought the people as well as their lands ; but that
does not mean that they became slaves, for there is not a
word concerning enforced labour, and the sole change was
that the government became the owner of the soil, and the
people the tenants, with this exception, that in the case of
the priests, for whom a royal provision had been already
made, there was no interference with their lands, and
no exaction required from them. At the same time that
this alteration was made in the tenure of the land, the
people, perhaps at first for reasons of simple convenience,
that they might be the more easily supplied from the
granaries, were brought into the cities, but afterwards,
probably from motives of state policy, and with a view to
the securing of greater centralisation, they were kept in
their city homes, and that, so far as appears, was the sole
permanent interference with their personal liberty. Now,
here again it is remarkable that the statements of the sacred
narrative are confirmed by those of secular historians.

Herodotus says that Sesostris divided the soil among
the inhabitants, assigning square plots of equal size to
all, and obtained his revenue from a rent paid annually by
the holders. Strabo affirms that the occupiers of land
held it subject to a rent ; and Diodorus represents the
land as possessed only by the priests, the king, and the
warriors. There is in Genesis no mention of the army,
the arrangement for them having been probably entered
into at a date subsequent to the time of Joseph, but in

regard to the other points there is entire harmony between the sacred and secular historians.* As to the state of things existing until very recent times in Egypt, the late Dr. Edward Robinson gives the result of his observation in the early part of 1838, in a passage from which I quote the following sentences, that I may point the contrast between the policy of Joseph and that of Mohammed Ali. He says, " By a single decree the pasha declared himself to be the sole owner of all the lands in Egypt, and the people of course became his tenants-at-will, or rather his slaves. It is interesting to compare this proceeding with a similar event in the ancient history of Egypt under the Pharaohs. At the entreaty of the people themselves Joseph bought them and their land for Pharaoh, so that ' the land became Pharaoh's '; but he gave them bread in return to sustain them and their families in time of famine. ' Only the land of the priests bought he not '; but the modern Pharaoh made no exception, and stripped the mosques and other religious and charitable institutions of their landed endowments as mercilessly as the rest.

" Joseph also gave the people seed to sow, and required for the king only a fifth of the produce, leaving four-fifths to them as their own property; but now, though seed is in like manner given out, yet every village is compelled to cultivate two-thirds of its lands with cotton and other articles solely for the pasha, and also to render back to him, in the form of taxes and exactions in kind, a large proportion of the produce of the remaining third." † The end of such a state of matters could only be a collapse like that which this generation has seen, and what may be the outcome of the present anomalous strife we may not foretell. This only we can say, things may be better,

---

* See " Speakers' Commentary," *in loco.*
† " Biblical Researches," vol. i. p. 29.

but they could hardly be worse.   The result, then, of
Joseph's prudence was, that the people were saved from
such terrible decimation as would inevitably have been
caused by famine, but that their lands were transferred to
the ownership of the government, and held by them as
tenants subject to an annual rental of one-fifth part of the
increase.

But now the inquiry suggests itself whether such a
policy was not oppressive and injurious, and on both
sides of that question much has been written, with great
ability, by different authors.   In such a discussion,
however, certain very important things have to be borne
in mind.   In the first place, the believer in the Divine
inspiration of the Scriptures is not bound to vindicate the
policy of Joseph in every particular.   The fact that a
thing is recorded in the Bible does not commit the author
of the Scriptures to its approval.   Many things are narrated, even regarding the servants of God, that are not
endorsed.   We need not specify examples, for they are
so numerous that pertinent illustrations will readily suggest
themselves to your remembrance ; but the existence of
such cases elsewhere relieves us from all anxiety as to the
conclusion which may be arrived at regarding Joseph's
administration here.   It may be a matter of curious
history, but even if it were proved to be unjust no good
argument could be drawn against the Bible because of
that.

It would be manifestly unfair to judge Joseph's policy
by the principles of modern political economy or by those
of New Testament enforcement and obligation.   We must
put him in the environment of his age, and we have no
right to expect from him conformity to a standard which
was not at that time in existence.

The policy itself was approved by those who had the
best means of judging of its character, and who, as being

directly and immediately concerned, would have felt its hardships, if there had been any in the case. But, so far from regarding him as an oppressor, the people hailed him as a benefactor, and said to him, " Thou hast saved our lives."

It must not be forgotten that Egypt is an exceptional country, and that, from the constant dependence of the people on the irrigation of their fields, and the continual changes made in the surface of the country by the annual inundation of the river, in the way of obliterating land marks, and removing part of the soil from the one side of the Nile to the other, the holding of all the lands by the crown would have special public advantages which could not well be either enjoyed or appreciated by the inhabitants of other territories. In conversation upon this subject with the venerable author of " The Land and the Book," I discovered that he was inclined to find the explanation of Joseph's settlement with the people for their lands in the unusual character of the country itself; and from what he then said I gathered that he would fully agree with Bishop Browne, when, in the " Speakers' Commentary," he alleges, " The peculiar nature of the land, its dependence on the overflow of the Nile, and the unthrifty habits of the cultivators, made it desirable to establish a system of centralisation, perhaps to introduce some general principle of irrigation, in modern phraseology, to promote the prosperity of the country by great government works, in preference to leaving all to the uncertainty of individual enterprise. If this were so, then the saying ' Thou hast saved our lives ' was no language of Eastern adulation, but the verdict of a grateful people."

For the rest, this policy of Joseph's did not create a scarcity for the advantage either of himself or of the monarch, but it provided the means of meeting a scarcity; it did not withhold corn, and so earn the curse of the

people, but it frankly brought it out as it was required,
and sold it at a price that was mutually agreed upon; it
did not insist on everything in the bond, no matter what
hardship might be thereby occasioned, for, so far as
appears, Joseph not only gave the people seed for their
fields, but also gave them back their cattle, which he had
meanwhile preserved to them; above all, it neither bought
what was not in existence nor sold what was not in actual
possession, and so it had in it nothing which makes it in
any respect a parallel case to those speculative combina-
tions among ourselves with which some have sought to
classify it.   True, it left the government owners of the
land, but, as we have seen, that was the most convenient
settlement both for the carrying out of systematic works
for the prevention of similar national calamities in the
future, and for the stoppage of all litigation over matters
of boundary; and one-fifth part of the produce, considering the fertility of the soil, was not an exorbitant rental,
especially if it included all government imposts of every
sort.   Indeed, that was the proportion required of the
Israelites by law at a later date in Canaan, for they had
to give one tithe to the Levites, and another to the sacri-
ficial feasts, and when they were foolish enough to set up
a king, they had to give still a third tithe to him, but they
never until after Solomon's day complained of hardship on
that score; therefore, all things considered, the arrangement made by Joseph with the Egyptians cannot be
called either unjust, oppressive, or in any way unstates-
manlike; and in England I have known many farmers
who would have desired nothing better than a long lease
on such terms as he granted the land to the people with
whom he had to do.

I have left myself but little space for any practical application of the principles illustrated in this interesting
history. But I must linger long enough to make at least

two remarks. Let us see how much we have to be thank-
ful for, in that for so many years we have enjoyed the
blessing of seed-time and harvest, and have been preserved from perils whether by fire or flood. These things
are in the Providence of God.

Some will tell us, indeed, that it is all a matter of law,
and that, if we will only conform to the requirements or
conditions in each case, we shall always have similar protection from the ravages of famine or of flood; but they
who reason in that way fail to take note of the fact that
there is always a region of uncertainty beyond the range
of human foresight, which God keeps entirely in His own
hand, and out of which there may come at any moment
some agency that may upset all our calculations, and
derange all our plans; and that, after all, because of that,
God is still supreme. Nay, more, as we saw in a former
chapter, the Providence of God is over human actions as
well as over physical laws; and so, look at it in any way
we may, we must still come to the conclusion that Jehovah
has been the author of our blessings.

How important is a good harvest to every branch of
trade and commerce in the country! and yet how seldom
we, especially we in the cities, think of recognising God's
hand in it! To be sure we have our Harvest Thanks-
giving-days, but it is only when some plague of insects,
or some long-continued drought comes over some large
section of the land, that we have the matter forced
upon our attention. When one member of the body
suffers, all the others suffer with it, and our sympathy
should take the practical form of rendering all needed
assistance. Glad am I to know that this has been so
largely the case, and that such prompt responses were sent
from our exchanges to the cries for help. " With such
sacrifices God is well pleased "; and at this particular
time it is well to remember that the fast which God has

chosen " is to loose the bands of wickedness, to undo the heavy burdens, and to let the oppressed go free ; to break every yoke, to deal bread to the hungry, to bring the poor that are cast out to thy house, and to cover the naked." That is practical gratitude to God shown by kindness to our fellow-men, and that is the sort of Lent and Thanksgiving we should keep all the round year, for the goodness of God in preserving us here from fire and flood and famine.

But, finally, we see how important it is to husband our resources in prosperity against the time of adversity. Joseph kept the surplus of the years of plenty and made it useful both to Pharaoh and his people in the years of famine ; and if the Egyptians generally had believed his warning and followed his example, they might not—indeed, we may say with all confidence, they would not—have been reduced to such straits as they were before the famine ended.   Now we ought to learn for ourselves to lay up in store against the time to come.   I know that the Saviour says we are to " take no thought for the morrow," but He means that we should not worry about to-morrow.   He never designed to rebuke prudence ; and, indeed, if there were more true prudence about the future with many, there would be less cause for anxiety in regard to it in their hearts.   To be prudent or provident, therefore, in saving from our surplus in time of plenty to meet a possible scarcity, is one of the best ways of obeying the Lord's command, " Be not anxious for the morrow."   Of course, I admit that the passion for hoarding is one of the most contemptible that can take possession of a human heart ; but I am not advocating hoarding.   For of his surplus the wise man will give a goodly proportion to God and His cause and to public charities, but he will be careful, also, to lay past a little for any contingency of sickness, or loss, or whatever else.   He who lives quite up to his income when that is at the largest, must suffer when, for any reason, it is lessened or entirely stopped. It is wise, therefore, always to live within one's means, so as to provide for what is popularly called "a rainy day." And when any exceptional prosperity comes we ought not to use that all up at once, but should store some of it, as Joseph did a portion of the harvest in the years of plenty. There is an old Scotch saying concerning those who, when a windfall comes, consume all the proceeds of it right off, and are reduced again straightway to poverty, that "it is either a hunger or a burst with them." And there are many among working-men, and young men beginning life, of whom I fear that is the truth. When they have it they make it go, and when they haven't it they have nothing. But God has no blessing for such improvidence. Look you ahead! and that you may meet the future better, save a little in the present.

And surely you will forgive me if, as I conclude, I beseech you in your outlook to take in eternity as well as time, and urge you to make some provision for that. Remember you have to pass away from earth; how important, therefore, it is, while you are on earth, to send something on before you! "Lay up for yourselves treasure in heaven," and seek to have there in store the true riches; or, as Paul has phrased it, "Do good, be rich in good works, ready to distribute, willing to communicate; laying up in store for yourselves a good foundation against the time to come, that ye may lay hold on eternal life." And as the beginning and root of all that, believe in the Lord Jesus Christ and build your life after His principles. You remember the story of the good old court-jester and his dying master. After some more than usually ridiculous outburst of his humour, the king had given him a beautiful staff, telling him to keep it until he found a greater fool than himself, and then to hand it to him. For years he carried the staff wherever he went, until it came to be regarded as his badge of office. But now the king was dying, and his affectionate old servant went in to visit him. The monarch said, " I am going a long journey"; whereupon the jester asked, " Has your majesty made any provision for the way?" to which the king replied, " No." " Does your majesty know where you are going? or have you made any arrangements for your reception at your destination?" "No," was still the answer. "Then, " said the faithful old man, with tears in his eyes and his voice quivering with emotion, " take back this staff, for in you I have found a greater fool than myself, since I have cared for all these things in reference to my own departure." It is a simple story, and carries its own application—let not the force of it be lost on any one of us.

VIII.

"CORN IN EGYPT."

GENESIS xlii. 1-38.

THE famine which pressed so sorely upon Egypt seems to have extended to some of the neighbouring countries. But though in the land of the Pharaohs its proximate cause was the failure of the Nile to rise to its accustomed height in its time of flood, we need not be surprised to find that it was felt in some surrounding districts which were not directly irrigated by the water of that river. For, as we saw in a former chapter, the annual inundations of the Nile are due to the swelling of its volume by the heavy summer rains among the mountains of Abyssinia, which wash down the rich lands of that region by the Blue Nile and the Atbara. Now, as these rains themselves are mainly the result of evaporation from the Mediterranean, the failure of that would equally affect the territories of Nubia, Arabia, and Canaan, which depend on the same thing for their water supply. And Dr. Kitto, in the "Pictorial Bible," tells us that "there are not wanting historical instances of years of dearth which were common to Egypt with the adjoining countries. Thus the historian Makrisi describes a famine which took place in Egypt on account of a deficiency in the increase of the Nile, in the year of the Hejira 444, which at the same time extended over Syria, and even to Bagdad."*

---

* Quoted in "Joseph and his Times," by Thornley Smith, p. 115.

A similar state of things existed in the case before us, and so the sufferers flocked to Egypt, that they might obtain relief by purchasing some of the stores which had been laid up there through the forethought of Joseph.

From some of these parties who had returned with their supplies to Canaan, Jacob, who had begun to feel the pressure of the general calamity, heard that there was "corn in Egypt," and, as the result of a family consultation, he sent his ten sons to that land, that they might obtain the food for the lack of which they were languishing—his *ten* sons, for he would not trust Benjamin to the care of the others. Not that Benjamin was still a child, for he must now have been between twenty and thirty years of age; but he was the son of his beloved Rachel, and since the disappearance, or, as Jacob had been led to believe, the death of Joseph, he had succeeded to the favoured place in his father's affections. He feared, therefore, lest some mischief should befall him, and so he determined to keep him by his side. Perhaps there had been through all these years a lingering suspicion in his mind that Joseph had met with some foul play at the hands of his brothers, and he did not choose to put Benjamin similarly in their power; or perhaps it was only the weak but pardonable partiality of a somewhat broken-hearted old man who had seen sore sorrow, and who clung to the presence of his youngest son because of the associations with "the days which were no more" that were so largely centred in him. But in any case he would not let Benjamin go. So the ten brothers set out from Hebron without him, and in due season arrived in Egypt, where they were ushered into the presence of the lord of the country. For though Joseph did not himself attend to the supply of the people of Egypt, it would appear that all applicants from other lands had to be subjected to his personal cross-examination. This is to be accounted for

by the extreme jealousy which the Egyptians had of all
foreigners, and which would naturally be stronger than
usual at a time when all the energies of the nation were
strained to the uttermost to meet the evil which was then
upon the people.

When Joseph saw the ten brothers he knew them in a
moment, but they did not recognise him. That was
perfectly natural, for when he was sold by them to the
Ishmaelites they had all attained to the maturity of manhood, and the twenty years or so which had intervened
would not have made much change on them, since from
thirty-five to fifty or fifty-five the alteration in a person's
appearance is not so great as that which occurs in the
same interval either before or after these two limits.
Besides, the ten were together, dressed in the same
fashion as of yore, and speaking the old mother-tongue.
But he had broadened out from the youth of seventeen to
the man of eight-and-thirty, was shaven after the manner
of the Egyptians, and was arrayed most likely in some
official robe, while he spoke to them through the medium
of an interpreter.

As they entered into his presence "they bowed themselves before him with their faces to the earth"; and we
can more easily imagine than describe the thrill that
tingled through his frame as now at length, in this
marvellous manner, he saw the fulfilment of his early
dream. How near he must have felt God to be in that
supreme moment! and yet to the onlooker how common-
place the whole scene appeared! How unconscious, too,
at the time, these ten men were that they were doing anything to verify their brother's dreams! and what a
commentary it all was on their mocking and malicious
words of long ago—"Behold! this dreamer cometh. Come
now, therefore, and let us slay him, and cast him into a
pit, and we will say an evil beast hath devoured him; and

we shall see what will become of his dreams!" And they did see, but the sight was very different from that which they had planned to make it. "Man proposes, but God disposes." He is always as near to us as He was to Joseph at this long-anticipated moment, and the common-place, if we had but the eyes to see, is as bright with His presence as is the unusual of the marvellous; while, through our own free agency, we are all the time unconsciously working out His purposes; for, as Isaac Taylor suggestively remarks, "This is the very miracle of Providence, that no miracles are needed for the carrying out of its designs." Every actor in this life-drama is seen working according to his own character, and acting according to his own unfettered will. No violence is done to the free agency of any one of them, and yet, in some inscrutable way, they all carry forward one great purpose, and the word of God is fulfilled. Thus God was in and over this history from first to last. But in that it was not in the least degree exceptional, for He is as really in each of our lives, and we shall miss the great moral of the story if we do not come to a clear recognition of that fact.

But now let us look for a little at Joseph's treatment of his brethren. As we have seen, he had them at a great disadvantage, for he knew them, but they did not know him, and he determined to avail himself of that for the testing of their characters. He had not yet formed any definite purpose as to his future disposal of them; there was, so far as appears, no idea in his mind at this time of bringing them all to reside permanently in Egypt; he simply wanted to find out what sort of men they now were, and whether they had anything like regret or repentance for their cruel treatment of himself. For this purpose he determined to preserve his *incognito* a little longer, and to act a part before them, or towards them, which might bring their sin to remembrance. You may remember how the great dramatist represents Hamlet as seeking "to catch the conscience of the king" by engaging the players to act in the royal presence a tragedy which should portray a murder, while he determined to watch the effect on his uncle. Now, much in the same way here, Joseph decided to be himself an actor, and to treat his brothers not according to his real nature, but in such a way as would particularly remind them of their conduct towards himself. Then, from the result, he would form his opinion of their characters and decide what he should do with them.

Some may think that he was blameworthy in all this, but so far as the mere representation of himself as being other than he really was is concerned, I cannot think of condemning him; for there was no malice in his heart, and his purpose was of the highest sort; nor can I forget that the Lord Himself did something of the same kind in His interview with the Syro-Phœnician woman. I cannot find great fault with Joseph, therefore, for seeking on this occasion to act a part which was not really natural to him, and if in one or two points he rather overdid it, we must not set that down to harshness, or anything like revenge, but rather to his inexperience as a hypocrite; for the transparentness of his disposition made it difficult for him to wear a disguise, and the very tenderness of his heart, strange as it may appear, contributed to the vehemence of his speech, for he had to make his manner rougher and his words coarser, just that he might be the better able to choke back his tears.

They had justified their cruelty to him by alleging that he had been a spy on their conduct, and had reported their evil deeds to their father; and so now, after asking whence they were, and receiving for answer that they had come from the land of Canaan to buy food, he most

abruptly and sternly accused them of having come to
Egypt on a hostile mission, to spy out the defenceless
character of the country on its north-eastern boundary,
and to carry back such a report as might tempt the
Canaanites to make an invasion at the time when the
people were suffering such privation from famine.   But
they indignantly and honestly repelled the charge, saying,
" We are all one man's sons; we are true men; thy
servants are no spies."   This was a good and sufficient
answer, for it showed that their mission was one of family
necessity, and not of national ambition.   But he reiterated
his accusation, and they replied with more explicitness,
" Thy servants are twelve brethren, the sons of one man
in the land of Canaan; and, behold, the youngest is this
day with our father, and one is not."   Ah! what subtle
suggestiveness is in these words, and how must they have
gone to the very depths of Joseph's heart long before the
interpreter had finished turning them into the language of
Egypt!   " One is not."   So they thought him dead; and
the very idea must have made " a lump in his throat."
But stay! what have we here?   " Thy servants are twelve
brethren, but one is not."   Is not that the very thought
with which Wordsworth has made us all so familiar in his
little ballad, " We are seven "?   Was it, therefore, that in
the Hebron home they still thought the family unbroken,
though they had given him up for dead?   Could it be
possible, in spite of all that had come and gone, that he
had such a place in their thoughts and in their hearts?
Then, " the youngest is this day with our father "; and so
Jacob was yet alive, and Benjamin was at home with him.
The news made a flutter at his heart, and in that way we
explain the broken, hurried impatience of his rejoinder,
and the assumed and exaggerated emphasis of his words,
which he had to help out with an Egyptian asseveration,
not once only but twice, making a show of force, as many

a general has done, simply to hide his weakness. "That is it that I spake unto you, saying, ye are spies: hereby ye shall be proved. By the life of Pharaoh ye shall not go forth hence, except your youngest brother come hither. Send one of you, and let him fetch your brother, and ye shall be kept in prison, that your words may be proved, whether there be any truth in you: or else by the life of Pharaoh surely ye are spies." And so he abruptly closed the interview by ordering them to be put all together into prison until they should accede to his terms.

They had put him into a pit, and now he put them into prison, and awaited the result. He allowed them to be thus shut up by themselves for three days, and then summoning them to his presence once more, he relented so far as to reverse his former proposal, and gave as the reason for his change of plan the fact that he feared God. This must have seemed a little strange to them, especially as he appeared to recognise their religious belief, and to place himself in the same category with them in that matter; but the terms which he now offered were so much better than those which he had at first laid down, that they lost sight of everything else for the moment, in their eagerness to accept his new proposal. Instead of insisting on sending only one of them to Canaan, and keeping the other nine as hostages for his return with Benjamin, he is willing now to let nine go and carry corn for the famine of their houses, while he kept one of them bound in prison as a pledge for their coming again with their youngest brother! It was hard enough still, but it was better than before, and making a virtue of necessity they agreed to do as he had said.

But which of them should be thus retained as a hostage for the rest? That was now the distressing question; and it was while they were still in suspense concerning it that they began to say one to another, " We are verily guilty concerning our brother, in that we saw the anguish of his soul, when

he besought us, and we would not hear; therefore is this distress come upon us." Now, when they are each facing lia-
bility to that isolation and loss of liberty to which they had
consigned Joseph, their sin against him is brought to their
remembrance, and by a simultaneous impulse they begin to
speak to each other of their guilt. They had shown no mercy
to him, and they need not be surprised, therefore, if now
no consideration should be had for them. But there was
one exception to this chorus of confession, for Reuben had
tried honestly, though perhaps not as watchfully and
persistently as he might, to save Joseph from his brothers'
rage; and so, while vindicating himself, he only put
another thorn into the consciences of the rest when he
said, "Spake I not unto you, saying, do not sin against
the child; and ye would not hear? therefore, behold, also
his blood is required." All this conversation was carried
on by them in a sort of "aside" and in the presence of
Joseph, without the least suspicion on their part that he
understood every word they said. The effect on him was
so great that he could not restrain his tears, and went
away for a little to conceal his emotion; for it was not
time yet to declare himself unto them, since he wanted
still to see how they treated Benjamin, and to that end it
was needful that he should maintain for some time longer
the character which he had assumed. So he took Simeon,
perhaps because he knew the harshness of his disposition
as manifested at Shechem, or, possibly, because Simeon
might have been the ringleader of the brothers in their
persecution of himself, and after binding him before their
eyes, gave orders that he should be taken to prison.
Then, commanding the servants in the granaries to give
the rest all the corn they desired, together with smaller
haversacks filled with provisions for the way, and to
restore every man's money into his sack, he sent them
back to Hebron.

On their arrival at their first resting-place for the night, one of them having occasion to open his sack of corn—not his travelling sack, but the larger bag which had not been designed to be disturbed until he reached home—found his money returned, and this discovery added greatly to their dismay. They feared that they were the victims of some conspiracy, and could not contemplate going back to Egypt without trepidation; but one good symptom in them was that now they began to think of the overruling Providence which before they had so greatly slighted; for they said, "What is this that God hath done unto us?"

On their arrival at Hebron, where perhaps they had been eagerly expected, not only because of the pressure of the famine, but also because of the delay in their return, they told their father all that had occurred between them and the lord—or Adon—of the land and how they had been compelled to leave Simeon behind them, with the assurance that his liberty could be secured only by their taking Benjamin with them when next they went for food. This was heavy news for Jacob; and when, on opening up their sacks, each one found that it was with him as with the brother at their first halting-place, and every man's bundle of money was restored, they were all alarmed. Joseph had meant it in kindness, but the sternness of his manner made his very kindness be suspected, and they thought it only some new trap for their ensnaring. It was on Jacob, however, that the blow fell with most severity, and he could think of nothing but his sons. So he sent forth this wail of sadness—"Me have ye bereaved of my children: Joseph is not, Simeon is not, and ye will take Benjamin away: all these things are against me." It was a bitter cry, not to be stayed by Reuben's impulsive words of promise to bring Benjamin back. Poor Jacob! how he would smile in after-years at this unnecessary anxiety! But it was very real to him then; and as he thought of his long-lost Joseph and the missing Simeon, we cannot wonder that he should say, with something of passionate vehemence concerning Benjamin, " My son shall not go down with you; for his brother is dead, and he is left alone: if mischief befall him by the way in the which ye go, then shall ye bring down my grey hairs with sorrow to the grave." What a mixed condition of affairs we often find on earth, and how many tears are shed that would never have wet our cheeks if we had known the true state of the case! Yet they are not useless tears because of that. Joseph weeps at the discovery of his brethren's penitence, and his heart is relieved by the vent thus given to his emotion; for it is more dangerous to restrain tears of joy than those of sorrow. Jacob weeps over the occurrence of an event which never happened, and the anticipation of an evil that never came; yet the sorrow in the end was salutary, for, like the shrinking of his limb at Peniel beneath the angel's touch, it threw his entire weight upon God, and he was upborne in the everlasting arms.

But now, leaving the deeply interesting narrative, and concentrating our attention for a little on this lamentation of Jacob, let us see what we may learn for ourselves from its consideration.

It was very natural for the patriarch to speak in this way ; and though we may not vindicate him for murmuring, we understand his state of heart too well to think of up-braiding him for giving way so far to the bitterness of his grief. " He that is without sin among you let him cast the first stone at him." I cannot. My heart is too full of pity for him, and I have too often been just like him, so I dare not chide his tears. But one thing surprises me in his ejaculation, and that is that he makes no mention of God. He speaks to his sons as if they had done it all, but he makes no reference to Him who said to him, on the memorable night at Bethel, " I am with thee, and will keep thee in all places whither thou goest." For the moment he has forgotten how the Lord had led him at first to Laban's house, and had given him prosperity during his twenty-one years' sojourn in Padan-aram; how He had cared for him when he left his father-in-law; how He had mollified for him the anger of Esau; how He had blessed him at Peniel after the night-long wrestle; and how He had protected him at the time when the violence of some of his sons might have drawn upon him the vengeance of the Shechemites. Now God was in this new trial as much and as really as He was in those old ones, and if Jacob had remembered that, he would not have spoken as he did. We shall see, indeed, that after a while, when his sons were bidding farewell on their departure for Egypt for more food, he came back to his old trustfulness, and offered for them his prayer : " God Almighty give you mercy before the man, that he may send away your other brother and Benjamin. If I be bereaved of my children, I am bereaved." But at the first, when the full shadow of his trouble passed over him, God was to him, for the moment, eclipsed, and that only made his trial heavier.

Then, besides being thus practically atheistic, this declaration of Jacob was ultimately found to be untrue. All these things were not against him. They were really working together for his good. They were onward steps in that process by which he was to recover his long-lost son, and was to have conferred upon him those years of happiness that, as we read the history, seem to us to be like the Sabbath of his earthly life, which after the labour and sorrow of the week he was enabled to spend in rest, in thankfulness, and in joy. How he would blame himself for these hasty words in those latter days, when he went to see Joseph in his palace, and took his grandsons between his knees; and I can imagine him saying to the

God of his fathers, after all the riddle of his life had been unfolded to him, " Now I know the thoughts of Thy heart towards me, and I bless Thee that they were thoughts of peace, and not of evil, to give me this delightful end."

Now, from this analysis of Jacob's experience, we may learn that God is in all the events of our lives. Many of us are ready enough to admit that He is in the prosperous things, but when trouble comes upon us we attribute that solely to others, and in that way we lose the comfort which otherwise we might have enjoyed under its endurance. The mercies of a lifetime are often ignored by us under the bitterness of a single trial; and God, who has been our friend for years, is forgotten altogether, while we passionately condemn some others as the authors of our affliction. But we shall never find consolation that way. The first thing we ought to say regarding every trial is, " It is the Lord." No matter what may have been the human instrumentality through which we may think our trouble has come upon us; no matter what may have been the material causes which have apparently operated against us—in and over all human actions and all material operations there is God. His providence is universal and supreme, and the first thought of our spirits should be, " It is the Lord." Then that will steady us; for did He not give His own Son to death for us on the Cross? Has He not shown His kindness to us in multitudinous and unmistakable ways throughout our lives? Can it be, therefore, that He means anything but good to us in anything, even though it should be a terrible affliction? Thus, so soon as we trace a trial up to God, we are on the way to comfort and support under it. For there are not two Gods —one of providence, and one of redemption. Jehovah is one, and He who " so loved the world that He gave His only-begotten Son, that whosoever believeth in Him should not perish, but have everlasting life," is at the

same time He who orders our lives and sends and super-
intends our affliction. We may, therefore, have absolute
faith in His goodness, not only *in spite of* trial, but *through*
trial. You remember how, after Manoah's sacrifice, when,
as the angel of the Lord did wondrously, the conviction
forced itself upon him that it was the Lord Himself, and
he said to his wife, " We shall surely die, because we have
seen the Lord," she re-assured him with these words : " If
the Lord were pleased to kill us He would not have
received a burnt-offering at our hands, neither would He
have shown us all these things ; nor would He, as at this
time, have told us such things as these." * Now the
argument I raise from the Cross of Christ here is similar
to that. If God had wished our destruction, or any
absolute evil to befall us, He needed not have sent His Son
to make atonement for our sins. But the very fact that He
has done that proves that He desires our highest welfare,
and will make all things subservient to our everlasting
good. Therefore, if we would not fall into despair under
our trials, let us recognise God's hand in them, and let us
think of Him as the God and Father of our Lord Jesus
Christ. The Cross of Christ is thus the healing tree which,
cast into the bitter waters of our trials, makes them sweet
and wholesome. If, instead of turning *on* his sons, Jacob
had only turned *to* his God, he would have been sustained ;
and we may be sure of this, that trouble never yet overwhelmed a man so long as he could see God in it.

Then, again, from our analysis of Jacob's case, we ought
to learn to pass no sentence of condemnation on God's
work until it is completed. " Judge nothing before the
time." We must not argue, from the pain of a part of the
process, that there is evil intended to us in the result of
the whole. The surgeon has a stern aspect, and apparently

---

* Judges xiii. 22, 23.

an unfeeling hand, when he cuts into the diseased organ or amputates the broken limb, but he is working towards healing all the time. And so it is with God and the discipline of His children. Wait until He finish His work before you condemn it. Wait until He finish His work, and when you can see the end from the beginning, as He has done all along, when you can look back upon the beginning from the end, and see His plan as a whole, you will not need that any one should vindicate His ways to you.

Finally, if these two things be true, that God is in our trials, and that the outcome of them all under His supervision will be good, we may surely stay ourselves in trouble by earnest prayer. " Is any among you afflicted, let him pray." We have to deal with no blind, remorseless law. The Lord Jesus has taught us to say " *Our Father*," and when we enter fully into the meaning of these words, and recognise clearly that His providence is universal, we shall have no difficulty in saying " *Thy* will be done "; for the Father's will is always love to His own children. That will sustain us while we are on earth. Then when we have passed from earth to heaven, and look back from the side of the throne above on all the way by which we were led here below, we shall feel much as Jacob must have felt in Egypt when he reviewed the incidents in his career, but only more intensely, and we shall be constrained to say, not "all these things were against me," but rather, " Now I know that all things wrought together for my good. My light afflictions, which were but for a moment, *have* wrought out for me a far more exceeding and eternal weight of glory."

IX

SECOND JOURNEY OF HIS BROTHERS TO EGYPT.

GENESIS xliii.-xlv. 15.

AS the story advances towards its climax of interest in Joseph's revelation of himself to his brethren, it grows in simplicity and pathos, so that one fears to touch it, lest he should mar its beauty by any attempt at paraphrase. It is, withal, so perfectly familiar to every reader of the Scriptures that little more is needed on our part than to mark the several steps in its ascent to that family re-union in which it culminates, and to account for which it has been introduced into the sacred narrative. Canaan was not yet ripe for the inheritance of the tribes, and the tribes had not yet that importance in numbers and resources which was needed for their entering upon its possession. They required time and opportunity for growth, and even after that they had to be put into the fire of trial, that they might be fused into a nation. For these purposes it was necessary that they should go down into Egypt and dwell there for many generations. The history of Joseph tells how that was brought about, and so it has its place in the Hebrew annals; while in itself it possesses, as we have seen, a thrilling interest of its own, and is fraught with lessons of great value for our modern life. But to get at these it is not needful to go into a minute recapitulation of its details, and we may, therefore, content ourselves with describing the different scenes, if so we may call them, in that act of the drama which forms our special subject at present.

The first is in the Hebron home of Jacob and his sons. The pressure of famine is again upon the encampment, and Jacob says to his sons, "Go again, buy us a little food." This is only what his sons have waited for. They knew that necessity would soon constrain him to accede to Joseph's terms, and therefore, after his first outburst of impatient opposition, they left him to his own reflections, and allowed him to take the initiative. But so soon as he opened up the subject again, Judah, who comes now to the front, and manifests the highest wisdom, and the greatest consideration for all parties concerned, took speech in hand. He reminded his father that it would be only making matters worse for them if they should return to Egypt without Benjamin, since that would be interpreted by the Egyptian lord as an evidence that they had spoken untruly on their former visit, and would probably end in the imprisonment of them all along with Simeon; so that, as the result, he would have neither food nor sons, save Benjamin only. And when his father petulantly asked why they had told the great man that they had another brother, he defended their conduct by describing how the information had, as it were, been forced out of them by the accusation that they were spies, and by the repeated interrogations of their questioner, consequent upon their statement that they were all sons of one man. This account seems at first slightly inconsistent with that given in the narrative of their first visit, but all discrepancy is removed by the remembrance of the fact that the history does not pretend to give a full report of all that passed at their interview with Joseph, so that there is no need to impute to Judah any falsification of the facts of the case.

There was no resisting the force of his words when he

asked, " Could we certainly know that he would say,
Bring your brother down ? " But the power of his
appeal, great as it was, was strengthened when, with
a noble spirit of self-sacrifice, he offered to become surety
for Benjamin's safety, and added, "except we had lingered,
surely now we had returned this second time." It is
curious to note how here the different individualities of
Reuben and Judah came out in their methods of dealing
with their father. Reuben, in his impetuous way, not
meaning the half of what he said, exclaimed, " Slay my
two sons if I bring him not to thee; deliver him into
my hand, and I will bring him to thee "; a perfectly
preposterous proposition, the very extravagance of which
betokened that he who made it was not to be trusted for
constancy, since such ardour could not last. Judah, however, put not his sons but himself in the gap ; and in that
Jacob saw the pledge not only of his sincerity, but also
of his determination at all hazards to make good his
promise. To him, therefore, his father yielded ; and
mindful of what gifts had formerly done to mollify his
brother Esau, Jacob recommended his sons to take with
them a present of such things as they had, and carry it
down to him whom they were all so desirous to propitiate.
This present consisted of some of the most famous productions of their country, such as the famine had still
left to them ; and in the description here given of their
gift there is incidental evidence of the straits to which
they were reduced—" a *little* balm, and a *little* honey,
spices and myrrh, nuts and almonds." Besides these
things Jacob commanded his sons to take with them
not only money enough for their new purchase, but also
that which had formerly been restored to them, lest there
should have been some mistake about it which might lead
to unpleasant consequences. Then, as they were starting,
with the son of Rachel under their care, the old piety of

Israel came out, as he looked reverently up and said, in mingled faith and resignation, " God Almighty give you mercy before the man, that he may send away your other brother, and Benjamin. If I be bereaved of my children, I am bereaved."

The scene now changes to Egypt. The brothers have arrived at the public storehouse to make their application for supplies. Joseph is in his office attending to his wonted business, and sees them in the street. With eager eye he scans the company, and discovers with a palpitating heart that Benjamin is with them. So, without waiting to converse with them, or even to receive them, he sends out his steward to take them to his house, and make all preparations for their dining with him at noon. It has been objected here that the narrator must be in error in representing Joseph as giving orders for the slaughter of animals for food, since that must have been contrary to the customs of the Egyptians; but Wilkinson, in describing preparations for dinner, says,* " an ox, kid, wild-goat, gazelle, or oryx, and a quantity of geese, widgeons, quails, or other birds were obtained for the occasion "; and Kalisch alleges† that " though there was scarcely an animal which was not held sacred in some province, there was, perhaps, with the only exception of the cow, none which was not eaten in other parts of the land "; so that the description here is in perfect harmony with what we now know to have been the habit of the people.

But the taking of the sons of Jacob to the house of Joseph was, at first, a source of perplexity to them. They could not understand for what purpose they were conducted thither. They were not informed of his hos-

---

* " Ancient Egyptians, vol. ii. p. 22.
† Quoted in " Pulpit Commentary," vol. i. p. 484.

pitable intent, and imagined that they were to be called
in question about the money which they had found in
their sacks on their return from their former visit; therefore they took the opportunity, as they were approaching
the palace, to make the steward acquainted with the true
state of the case. But as soon as he understood the
nature of their anxiety, he reassured them by telling them
in the kindest manner that he had received their money
and knew all about it, and by bringing Simeon out to
them that they might be all united once again. One
cannot but marvel at the spirit manifested by this servant.
He seems, indeed, to have been taken by his master into
his confidence for the occasion, and the words which he
uses would indicate either that Joseph had told him
precisely what to say, or that he was himself, under the
influence and example of Joseph, a believer in Jehovah;
for thus he speaks: " Peace be to you, fear not: your
God, and the God of your father, hath given you treasure
in your sacks: I had your money."

Surely now, therefore, they would be set at rest, for was
not this an answer to their father's prayer, " God Almighty
give you mercy before the man"? That impression would
be deepened when they saw that the steward treated them
as his master's guests, and gave them water for their feet
and provender for their asses, telling them at the same
time that they should eat bread there. So they got their
present ready, and when Joseph came they put it into his
hands and bowed themselves to the earth, thus once again
fulfilling the dream of his youth. Then came the question,
" Is your father well, the old man of whom ye spake?
Is he yet alive?" and once more they made obeisance
with the answer, " Thy servant our father is in good
health, he is yet alive," thus uniting their father in their
homage at his feet. But when he saw Benjamin, it was
a little more than he could do to keep up the part which

he had been studiously acting, and without waiting for an answer to his inquiry, "Is this your younger brother, of whom ye spake unto me?" he said, with the deepest feeling, "God be gracious unto thee, my son," and hastened into his chamber to hide the tears which he could no longer restrain. Then, after having given way for a season to his uncontrollable emotion, he washed his face to remove all traces of his weeping, and went back to preside over the banquet which he had caused to be prepared for them.

The next scene, therefore, is in the dining-hall. Joseph sits by himself; the Egyptians of his household are seated by themselves; and the eleven brothers by themselves, yet not indiscriminately; for, somewhat to their amazement, and tending, no doubt, to deepen the mystery of their reception, he caused them to be placed in the order of their age—"the first-born according to his birthright, and the youngest according to his youth." And now he begins that testing ordeal to which, all unknown to them, he designed to submit his half-brothers. They had been jealous of him in the olden time because his father had shown a partiality for him, and they had preferred their own indulgence to his welfare, selling him into slavery rather than give up their evil courses. He determines now, therefore, to see whether they have the same disposition towards Benjamin. If they have, he will keep Benjamin in Egypt along with himself; but if they have not, then the door may be opened for bringing all his brethren and his father with them, to sojourn in the land of plenty. That, as it seems to me, is the key to the explanation of all his after-dealings with them. He commences by sending to Benjamin a portion from that which was before him, five times larger than that which he had sent to any of the others. That was a mark of his preference, almost as great as his father had shown him in giving him the coat of many colours; and from what happened when Elkanah gave to Hannah "a worthy portion," thereby provoking Peninnah to jealousy,* we may be sure that if they had been envious of Benjamin they would have revealed it by their remarks upon his procedure. But no such manifestation was made by them, and the feast was one of harmonious gladness, betokening that all were delighted with his hospitality, "for they drank and were merry with him."

But now the scene changes once again. It is the early morning, and they are all up and eager to start for home. Before they had arisen, the steward, by Joseph's orders, had filled their sacks with corn, and had put every man's money into his sack's mouth, and along with that a silver cup of a peculiar description in the sack of Benjamin. And now everything being ready for their departure, they set out upon their asses, Judah's heart beating with especial joy that Benjamin was riding by his side. But they had scarcely cleared the city when they were overtaken by the steward, who accused them of having stolen a valuable cup. "Wherefore," said he, "have ye rewarded evil for good? Is not this it in which my lord drinketh, and whereby indeed he divineth?" A great deal has been made of this expression, and of Joseph's own words later, "Wot ye not that such a man as I can certainly divine?" but the sum of the matter seems to be this: the Egyptians did practise divination by cups. How that was done is not now certainly known, but according to some authorities a liquid was poured into a saucer-shaped vase, and from the reflections on its surface various conclusions were drawn. Now, from what Joseph said to Pharaoh about the interpretation of his dreams, we have not only no reason to believe that he was guilty of any

---

* 1 Samuel i. 4-8.

such deceit as to attempt to foretell the future, or to reveal the unknown by any such means, but, rather, every reason to believe that he would have repudiated such folly. Just now, however, he is acting a part, and he adapts himself and his language to the character which he has assumed. That he was perfectly justified in preserving his *incognito* I have little doubt, but whether or not he here rather overdid his acting may be a matter of question. Still, that he might do even that without giving countenance to divination is abundantly clear.

When the steward thus intercepted the brothers they were greatly disconcerted, and, conscious of their innocence, they offered to submit themselves to search, saying, " With whomsoever of thy servants the cup is found, both let him die, and we also will be my lord's bondmen." But with great apparent fairness he replied, " He with whom it is found shall be my servant: and ye shall be blameless." So the search proceeded, and, to their dismay, " the cup was found in Benjamin's sack." But they would not give him up alone, and returned with him to Joseph's house, with their clothes rent and their hearts heavy, to see what could be done. When Joseph upbraided them for their ingratitude, Judah, unable to contradict the evidence which had been brought against them, and with no word of blame for Benjamin—a thing which in the circumstances was most remarkable, and speaks much for his confidence in his younger brother—said, with great simplicity, " What shall we say unto my lord ? what shall we speak ? or how shall we clear ourselves ? God hath found out the iniquity of thy servants: behold, we are my lord's servants, both we and he also with whom the cup is found." But Joseph would not hear of any such injustice. The rest might go home, and the guilty one alone should be retained. That was his decision. Then Judah stood forward and pleaded the cause of Benjamin, in an appeal which for simple pathos, and that natural eloquence which, "when unadorned" is "adorned the most," is unsurpassed either in sacred or secular literature, whether of ancient or modern times. No summary can do it justice, and every variation from it would only mar its beauty; therefore I will simply read it, that you may feel its force :

" O my lord, let thy servant, I pray thee, speak a word in my lord's ears, and let not thine anger burn against thy servant : for thou *art* even as Pharaoh. My lord asked his servants, saying, Have ye a father, or a brother? And we said unto my lord, We have a father, an old man, and a child of his old age, a little one; and his brother is dead, and he alone is left of his mother, and his father loveth him. And thou saidst unto thy servants, Bring him down unto me, that I may set mine eyes upon him. And we said unto my lord, The lad cannot leave his father : for *if* he should leave his father, *his father* would die. And thou saidst unto thy servants, Except your youngest brother come down with you, ye shall see my face no more. And it came to pass when we came up unto thy servant my father, we told him the words of my lord. And our father said, Go again, *and* buy us a little food. And we said, We cannot go down : if our youngest brother be with us, then will we go down : for we may not see the man's face, except our youngest brother *be* with us. And thy servant my father said unto us, Ye know that my wife bare me two *sons:* And the one went out from me, and I said, Surely he is torn in pieces ; and I saw him not since : And if ye take this also from me, and mischief befall him, ye shall bring down my grey hairs with sorrow to the grave. Now, therefore, when I come to thy servant my father, and the lad *be* not with us ; seeing that his life is bound up in the lad's life ; It shall come to pass, when he seeth that the lad *is* not *with us*, that he will die : and thy servants shall bring down the grey hairs of thy servant our father with sorrow to the grave. For thy servant became surety for the lad unto my father, saying, If I bring him not unto thee, then I shall bear the blame to my father for ever. Now therefore, I pray thee, let thy servant abide instead of the lad a bondman to my lord; and let the lad go up with his brethren. For how shall I go up to my father, and the lad *be* not with me? lest peradventure I see the evil that shall come on my father."*

---

* Genesis xliv. 18-34.

Even if Joseph had been only an Egyptian magnate
such an intercession must have gained its end, but, being
the man he was, it moved his soul to the very depths. It
showed him that his brothers were not only sorrow for
what they had done to him, but were so changed that
now they could be trusted by him implicitly. Their
penitence had been proved to be sincere by their conduct.
Therefore, there and then, he gave up all idea of detaining
Benjamin, and resolved to make himself known to them,
and invite them and their families and his father to take
up their abode in Egypt. So with a full heart he caused
every one to leave his presence save themselves, and then,
with no spectators to mar the confidences of the interview,
he told them who he was, and how it had been with him.
He asked again after his father; and when he saw that
they were troubled lest he should seek to punish them for
their unkindness to him, he led their thoughts up to the
Providence which had overruled their evil for the good of
a whole nation, and for the welfare of their father's house.
Then, after sending a warm request to Jacob to come and
see all his glory in Egypt, he turned to Benjamin, and fell
upon his neck and wept. " Moreover, he kissed all his
brethren, and wept upon them, and after that his brethren
talked with him." How natural it all is! How exquisitely
told! and how remarkable that there should be no effort
on the part of the narrator to describe the surprise of the
brothers at the unexpected revelation, or to recount the
conversation which followed on the reconciliation!

And this is the sort of narrative which we are to believe
is a poetic fable, with no more foundation on fact than
one of the myths of Grecian literature, or the pre-historic
stories that are told about the founders of ancient Rome!
I am willing to put the two side by side, and await the
verdict of any candid investigator as to the internal
evidence of their relative veracity. But I must leave the

sequel of the recognition, and the details of the message to Jacob, for another chapter, while I turn now to pick up a few lessons from the interesting chapters over which we have come.

We may see, then, that fear misinterprets kindness. When the brothers were taken to Joseph's house, they at once concluded that some evil was intended for them, and began to excuse themselves to the steward about the money which they had found in their sacks, telling him at the same time that they had brought it with them again, and were ready to restore it to Joseph, to whom it rightfully belonged. But how were all such suspicions rebuked when they learned that they were to dine at his house! and how utterly ridiculous they would seem, at length, when they found out that he was their brother! But is it not just similar with the sinner and his God? He is afraid of the Lord, and that leads him to misinterpret all His dealings with him. When he is asked into God's house, he supposes it must be just that he may be made miserable; and when the Lord makes to him overtures of love they seem to him to be but the precursors of punishment. All this is because he has not yet discovered that God is his Father and Christ his elder Brother. When the day comes that Jehovah shall thus reveal Himself to him, there will be a weeping like that of Joseph here, but it will be all on his side; and the fear which persistently made him misunderstand God's dealings will be cast out by perfect love. The Gospel feast is prepared. All things are ready; and as one of the stewards of my Lord's house, I am come to lead you to His palace, that you may feast with Him. Be not afraid. He is your Father, and Christ is your Brother; therefore, stand not hesitatingly and tremblingly without, but take your places at His banquet, and rejoice in His salvation.

We may see here that we are often being tested while

we are unconscious of the fact that we are so. The whole
treatment of his brothers by Joseph was meant to prove
their characters, and see whether they had or had not repented of their sin against him, and whether they had or
had not changed their disposition and mode of life. They
did not know that he was thus experimenting on them, but
the result satisfied him, and led to his revelation of himself to them. Now, it is often similar with men and their
fellows. When Gideon led his army to the brook, and
saw his soldiers drink, they had no idea that he was pick-
ing out his three hundred for his midnight attack on the
Midianitish camp. But so it was ; for those who did not
care luxuriously to go down on hands and knees to put
their mouths to the stream, but who simply lapped the
water up with their hands as a dog laps with his tongue,
showed thereby that they had the qualities of rapidity,
dash, and hardihood which were specially needed for the
service on which he was bent, and, therefore, they were
selected for it. Even so men have been watched by
others when they were not thinking of anything of the
kind, and the diligence, energy, integrity, and amiability
which they have shown has commended them to those
interested for some situation of trust, honour, and emolument. Young man, your employer is testing you when
you do not know it, therefore see·that you are faithful and
obliging even in that which is least, that you may approve
yourself worthy of something greater.

Many incidents might here be narrated to prove that
men have risen from comparative obscurity to eminence
simply because they had been tested, unwittingly to themselves, by others who were on the outlook for the agents
that would most effectually serve their purpose. When
they rose, envious people prated about "luck," but they
who knew best spoke about character manifested by faith-
fulness in that which was least, and saw in their promo-

tion the earthly miniature of the doing of the last Judge, who shall say to him whom He approves, "Thou hast been faithful over a few things, I will make thee ruler over many things, enter thou into the joy of thy Lord." Nay, does not the very quotation which I have just made remind us that it is in the same way, and while we are unconscious of it, that the Lord tests those who are to come before Him at the last. He will say to those on His right hand, " I was an hungered and ye gave Me meat"; and they will exclaim in astonishment, " Lord, when saw we Thee an hungered and gave Thee meat?" He will say to those on His left hand, " I was an hungered and ye gave Me no meat "; and they will cry out amazed, " When saw we Thee an hungered and gave Thee no meat ? " They had not been conscious that they were undergoing a testing process, and yet by that their characters were judged, even as here Joseph gauges the feelings of the brothers towards Benjamin, by the little thing of sending to him a portion five times larger than each of theirs. Oh, my readers, we are being tested when we know not of it ! how important, therefore, that we do *everything*, small as well as great, in the name of the Lord Jesus.

But we have in this history an illustration of the difference between the outer appearance and the inner life of a man. Joseph externally was a stranger to his brothers, but internally his heart, latterly at least, was yearning over them, and he had once and again to retire to his chamber to give vent to his tears. But is he not herein very like most men at some time or other in their lives ? Go down to-morrow to the stores and examine the faces of those whom you find in them. Some will look calm and composed, almost marbly in their impassivity. Others may look jovial—ever and anon a ringing laugh comes from the corner where their desks are, and you call them cheerful. Yes ; but that is only the outward appearance. Suppose you could uncover the heart of each, what a contrast to the calmness, in the one case, and the joyousness, in the other, you might discover! Suppose you knew the entire life of each, how often you might find them both retiring to their chambers to weep! The proverb says that " there is a skeleton in every house," and it is equally true that there is a secret chamber in every heart where the soul keeps it skeleton, and to which, when it can no longer control itself, it retires to weep. What is in that secret chamber? It may be the memory of some sin ; it may be a hidden cross of such a nature that it can be described to no mortal; it may be—but why should I probe into those things with which a stranger may not intermeddle? Each of you knows his own, and whatever yours may be, my friend, take it to Christ. Give Him your confidence, and you will find how true the exquisite hymn of Horatius Bonar is when it says—

> I lay my griefs on Jesus,
>   My burdens and my cares;
> He from them all releases,
>   He all my sorrow bears."

But I must not be one-sided here. There is a joy which is a secret in the heart as well as a sorrow, and the Christian knows something of that. Eternally his life may be dull, commonplace, routine. There may seem nothing very particular about himself, but there is hidden sweetness in his soul. He is at peace with God, and *that* takes him every now and then into his chamber, not to weep, but to sing. He " carries music in his heart," and no matter how prosaic or hum-drum to outward appearance his life may be, that gives it a poetry that is peculiarly its own. Do you know anything of such an experience as that? If you do, it is a foretaste and earnest of the " white-stone," with the new name written

in it, " which no man knoweth save he that receiveth it."
It is the beginning of your heaven.

Finally, how can we read this touching appeal of Judah
for Benjamin without being reminded of Christ's intercession for us? The Lord Jesus not only offered to
become our surety, but was accepted as such, and now,
having offered Himself in sacrifice in the tabernacle court
—which is this lower world—He has entered through the
veil into the heavenly Holy of Holies, where He maketh
intercession for us. His intercession takes in all who
come unto God by Him, and yet it takes in everything
about each of them. Judah's plea had a powerful ally in
Joseph's love, and in the same way the intercession of
Jesus is sure of success for us, for the love of God is
already on our side ; therefore let us have perfect confidence that He will " bring to pass that which is good for
us, and make perfect that which concerneth us." O
sinner, arraigned before God's bar, and conscious of your
guilt, commit your case to this Surety, Sacrifice, and
Advocate all in one, and He will secure not only your
acquittal, but your acceptance—your salvation.

X.

JACOB AND HIS SONS REMOVE TO EGYPT.

GENESIS xlv. 16; xlvi. 1-6, 28-34; xlvii. 1-10.

IN the interests of brevity we were constrained, in our last chapter, to pass very lightly over two things that came out in Joseph's interview of reconciliation with his brethren, and it may be well to go back upon them for a few moments now. The first is his magnanimity towards them. He saw that they had fully repented of their sin against him, and therefore, when he observed that they were troubled at his presence, he said to them, "Be not grieved, nor angry with yourselves, that ye sold me hither: for God did send me before you to preserve life. For these two years hath the famine been in the land: and yet there are five years, in the which there shall neither be earing nor harvest. And God sent me before you to preserve you a posterity in the earth, and to save your lives by a great deliverance." Had they not been really penitent it might have been dangerous to preach such doctrine to them. But they had come to hate their sin, and were now in such a state of mind regarding it as to be verging towards despair, so that they required to be encouraged and comforted. And nothing could have been better calculated to lift them out of their despondency than the presentation of this aspect of the Divine providence. It did not make their guilt less serious, but it did make God more attractive.

As one has very epigrammatically expressed it, "God does not need our sins to work out His good intentions, but we give Him little other material; and the discovery that through our evil purposes and injurious deeds God has worked out His beneficent will, is certainly not calculated to make us think more lightly of our sins, or more highly of ourselves."* It only shows that a holy and loving God has been watching over us, and, therefore, strengthens the new bond between us and Him which our penitence has made. To say to a hardened, reckless man that God will overrule his sin for some good end, will only make him more regardless than ever. But when a man is truly penitent, and seems almost paralyzed by the perception of his guilt, to show him that God has brought good out of his guilt will exalt God's grace and wisdom in his eyes, and lead him more implicitly to cling to Him. It *is* a comforting thought, that while we cannot undo the sin, God has kept it from undoing us, and has overruled it for greater good to ourselves and greater blessing to others than, perhaps, might otherwise have been attained. We can never be as we were before we committed it. Always there will be some sadness in our hearts and lives connected with it, and springing out of it. But still, if we really repent of it and return to God, there may come to us "meat out of the eater, and sweet out of the bitter." It may give us sympathy with others, and fit us for being helpful to others, so that, though we may be sadly conscious of the evil of our course, we may yet see that through it all God was preparing us for the saving of those who, humanly speaking, but for our instrumentality would have gone down to perdition. But mark the condition—if we truly repent. There is no comfort otherwise; but that being secured, then the penitent may take into consolation, that out of his worst

---

* Dod's "Isaac, Jacob, and Joseph," p. 245.

sin God can and may bring good both to himself and others, and he ought to look for the means of bringing that about.

But the second thing in this interview on which I wish now to remark is the tender regard of Joseph for his father. Whatever may have been the reason for his not communicating with Jacob for so many years, we see that now there is no lack of filial affection in his heart. It was the pathetic reference of Judah to the probable result of Benjamin's detention on his father that fairly broke him down and opened up the fountain of his tears. Again and again he inquired after the old man's welfare. He seemed impatient now to see his face again, and urged his brothers to hasten home and tell the tidings " that he is alive and well, and lord over all Egypt." He sent also a very pressing and affectionate invitation to his father to come and sojourn near him ; and with the absolute assurance that Pharaoh would give him everything he chose to ask for his kindred, as well as with a view to their happiness and prosperity, he promised that they should dwell in the land of Goshen. It would seem, therefore, that the love which had been so long pent up had only gathered strength by being repressed, so that when it found vent again it flowed forth with more fervour and intensity than ever. Across the gulf of many years memory leaped as with a bound, and he was once more a boy again, basking in his father's affection. Then he was the ward of his parent, but now he would repay the kindness by becoming Jacob's protector ; and no difference in rank or station between them would keep him from enjoying the privileges and performing the duties of a son. A ruler to the Egyptians, he was and would still be a son to Jacob ; for he carried to his throne, unsophisticated and unaltered, the heart that beat beneath the coat of many colours. He was not ashamed of his father, but the greatest joy of his exaltation was that he

was thereby enabled to make provision for the wants of
Jacob's declining years.   There is a worthy example,
young men, for you.   Never lose your pride in your
parents or your love for them.   Never think of slighting
their poverty in the days of your prosperity; but share
your honours with them, and give them if you can the
pride of seeing you in "all your glory."

But now resuming the narrative, we need not wonder
that the recognition of his brothers by Joseph became
speedily known to those who were about him.   Oriental
emotion is demonstrative, and the sounds of weeping
coming from the chamber in which they were would lead
to curious inquiries as to its cause.   Very soon, therefore,
the news reached the ears of Pharaoh that Joseph's
brethren were come, and the monarch gave such orders
as showed how highly he valued his servant, and how
glad he was of the opportunity of doing him a kindness.
After consultation, as we may presume, with Joseph himself, he bade the brothers load their beasts and return at
once to Canaan; he invited their father, themselves, and
their households to return and sojourn in Egypt; he
promised that they should eat the fat of the land; he
gave them waggons for the removal of their belongings;
and to all these gifts Joseph added changes of raiment
for each of his half-brothers, but five changes of raiment
and three hundred pieces of silver for Benjamin.   Then
"to his father he sent ten asses laden with the good
things of Egypt, and ten she-asses laden with corn and
bread and meat for his father by the way."   So he
despatched them on their journey, giving them this
parting admonition, "See that ye fall not out by the way."

How well he knew human nature!   They were going
home with news which would reveal to their father that
they had been the cause of their brother's disappearance, and had imposed on him with a deliberate falsehood

and, for anything they knew, he might turn upon them and upbraid them with their cruelty and deceit. What so likely, therefore, as that they should begin to accuse each other—that crimination should lead to recrimination, and words to blows? Reuben might say again, " It was not my fault, for I sought to save his life, and I went back to the pit hoping to find him and restore him to our father." Judah might respond, " But for me he would have died, and it is to my happy suggestion to sell him to the Ishmaelites that we are indebted for all the good fortune that seems now to be coming to us "; while the rest, conscious of their share in the nefarious transaction, might have sought to still the upbraidings of their consciences by uttering bitter things against each other. All that might have happened on their journey home, and so Joseph was not giving unnecessary counsel when he said, " See that ye fall not out by the way." And they heeded his advice, for they reached home in peace; and it may be that, so far from quarrelling, they spent some of their time as they rode in conversing on the marvellous manner in which, in spite of their antagonism, and without their consciousness of anything in the least degree out of the way, the dreams of their brother had been fulfilled, and they had done obeisance at his feet.

When they arrived at Hebron and told the news to their father, he was utterly overwhelmed. He could not believe their words. On their own showing, they had deceived him before; what ground had he for assurance that they were not deceiving him again? It was a strange experience. He was in a place where two seas met, and he was well-nigh submerged by the violence of the waves. If they spoke truly, then he might yet see his long-lost son; but all these years his other children had been guilty of the blackest deceit, and was he to lose them in the finding of their brother? or was he to have them all thoroughly restored to him as brothers indeed? Surely they could not wantonly play with his feelings a second time? And yet, were not their tidings too good to be true? In this uncertainty—just as when a balance is on the turn a very little thing will give it impulse—the sight of the waggons gave the relief he needed, and the old Israel energy flamed forth, so that he said, " It is enough ; Joseph my son is yet alive : I will go and see him before I die." But what was there in the sight of the waggons to corroborate their tidings? The answer may be given in the words of Thornley Smith : * " It is probable that waggons were at that time not known in Palestine, whence Jacob inferred that these waggons had been sent from Egypt, where his sons could not have obtained them but in the manner they stated. A common kind of waggon having two wheels has been found depicted on some of the monuments ; but these were no doubt of a superior description, and being covered to screen the travellers from the sun, as we may presume they were, would be somewhat similar to the tilted waggons of modern times."

Convinced thus of the good faith of his sons, Jacob speedily made all preparations, and set out with his whole encampment from Hebron for the land of Egypt. But it was not without misgivings that he was taking this important step. He had a peculiar interest in the land of Canaan. It had been promised to him and to his children by God in covenant. Twenty-one years of his life had been spent outside of its borders, and he had come back to it again with new assurances that it was yet to be his own. It was therefore, in spite of the attraction that he was going to meet Joseph, a great trial to him to leave the Land of Promise. Besides, it had in it the Cave of Machpelah, where the bodies of his father and

---

* " Joseph and his Times," p. 167.

his grandfather had been laid, and he felt it hard to leave them behind. Nor was this all. Egypt had been an unpropitious place, apparently, both to Isaac and to Abraham, for each of them, during a brief sojourn there, had come into collision with its king, and it seemed almost as if it would not be safe for him—even with Joseph so near the throne—to venture within its borders. It was, we may suppose, with such feelings as these that Jacob found himself, in the course of his journey, at Beersheba. That was a well on the very edge of Canaan, just where it merges into the desert, and the place was dear to Jacob for its associations both with his father and with Abraham. There Abraham had planted a grove, and called upon the name of the Lord, the Everlasting God, and there Isaac had his encampment for many years; thence, too, it was that Jacob went out to begin his wanderings on the morning of that day whose evening was brightened for him at Bethel by the vision of the ladder and the angels. Naturally, therefore, his thoughts at that place were with his fathers and his fathers' God; and considering the nature of the journey which he was taking, we are not surprised to learn that there " he offered sacrifices to the God of his father Isaac." He made supplication to the Lord through sacrifice, and with special reference to the circumstances in which he was at the moment placed. Nor did he consult God in vain: for in the visions of the night the Lord said to him, " I am God, the God of thy father: fear not to go down into Egypt; for I will there make of thee a great nation. I will go down with thee into Egypt; and I will also surely bring thee up again; and Joseph shall put his hand upon thine eyes." Thus re-assured, he rose and resumed his journey, and when they drew nigh to their destination he sent Judah on before to apprise Joseph of their arrival, and to ask for instructions from his lips.

But when Joseph heard of his father's approach he went out himself to meet him, and when they saw each other " he fell on his father's neck, and wept on his neck a good while." Joseph's heart was too full for words, and when at length his father could command himself sufficiently for speech, it was but to say, " It is enough ; now let me die, since I have seen thy face, because thou art yet alive." After these salutations Joseph gave his brothers plain directions as to what they should say to Pharaoh on their introduction to the monarch. He anticipated that the king would ask them what their occupation was, and he told them to reply that they were shepherds, because that was true, and because he knew that such a confession would secure them a settlement away from the other inhabitants, in a district in which they could hold themselves aloof, not only from entangling alliances with the people, but also from contamination by the idolatries of the land : for " every shepherd is an abomination unto the Egyptians." This prejudice, however, was not owing to any hatred of the Hyksos or Shepherd dynasty that was now upon the throne, but rather to a deep-rooted spirit of caste among the people themselves. Herodotus tells us that the swine-herds—one of the seven classes into which the Egyptians were divided—were regarded with such abhorrence that they were not allowed to enter a temple or contract marriage with any others of their countrymen, and Wilkinson* testifies that pastors and shepherds were a class apart from the peasantry, and were held in such disrepute that the artists, as if to show their contempt, have represented them upon the monuments as lame or deformed, as dirty and unshaven, and sometimes of a most ludicrous appearance. From the very character of their country the Egyptians were essentially an agricultural

* " The Ancient Egyptians," vol. i. p. 289, and vol. iii. p. 444.

people, and as such they associated ideas of rudeness and
barbarism with those who, like shepherds, followed a
wandering life.   It may be, also, that part of their prejudice was due to the fact that shepherds were accustomed
to kill animals that were regarded as sacred by other
classes of the community.   But, whatever may have been
the reason for such sentiments, Joseph did not wish his
brethren to be exposed to the contempt with which he
knew the Egyptians would treat them as shepherds, and
he sought at the same time to turn their occupation to
their advantage by securing for them the very eligible
territory of the land of Goshen.

   That was a region lying to the north-east of Lower
Egypt, bounded on the north by the Mediterranean, on
the east by the desert, on the west by the Tanitic branch
of the Nile, and probably extending on the south as far as
to the head of the Red Sea.   It was under the dominion
of the Pharaohs, and therefore in Egypt, though it was
scarcely of it, for it was little more than on the confines
of the country.   It is called elsewhere the land of Rameses,
and under the Pharaoh of the oppression the Israelites
built in it the treasure-cities of Pithom and Rameses.   It was
a land of pasturage, suitable for the feeding of flocks, and
both for that reason and because it was nearest to Palestine,
and yet not far from his own residence, Joseph regarded it
as most advantageous for the members of his father's family.

   When, therefore, he took some of his brothers and
presented them to Pharaoh, they followed closely his
instructions, and went so far as to ask that, because of
their occupation and for the sake of their flocks, they
might be permitted to settle in Goshen.   This request was
instantly granted, and Joseph was commanded, if he should
see fit, and if he knew that any of them were qualified
for the office, to give them the charge of the royal herds.

   Then, after their audience was over, he led his venerable

father, with pride and affection, into the royal presence, and presented him to Pharaoh.   It was a memorable interview.   The greatest monarch of the time, the ablest statesman of his age, who was steadily steering Egypt through the fearful calamity of famine, and the oldest saint then upon the earth, heir to the promises made by God to Abraham and Isaac, were here brought into closest contact.   Never before or since has such a trio met, and we cannot read the account of the interview without remarking how true religion glorifies the common-place and lifts it up into a region that is literally sublime. One sees something of the same thing in what have been called the familiar personal epistles of the New Testament, namely, the letter of Paul to Philemon, and those of John to Gaius and the Elect Lady ; for in the former the sending of a request for favour to Onesimus, and in the latter the transmission of an ordinary friendly communi-cation, are made vital and luminous both with faith and holiness.   They all conform to the common forms of epistolary correspondence that were in use at the time, and yet they all fill these forms with living Christianity. So here Jacob comes before Pharaoh with the respect that was ordinarily given to a monarch ; but how differ-ently does that respect express itself in his case from those of ordinary presentations at court.   He begins and ends the interview with a benediction.   He does not hide his faith from the king, but he manifests it in such a way as to make it minister to the royal welfare by asking for him the favour of the Most High.   He who had seen God face to face, and who had come to Egypt with the assurance that God would accompany him, is not abashed before royalty ; but he does not presume, either, because of that, and therefore he shows his piety, not by admonition, but by benediction.   Then when the monarch asked the question most natural in the circumstances, " How old art thou ? "

He made this most significant reply : " The days of the
years of my pilgrimage are a hundred and thirty years:
few and evil have the days of the years of my life been,
and have not attained unto the days of the years of the
life of my fathers in the days of their pilgrimage." This
was one of the occasions referred to by the author of the
Epistle to the Hebrews, in which the patriarchs " confessed that they were strangers and pilgrims." It was
very true of the past of Jacob's life that it had been a
pilgrimage, for he had been twenty-one years a stranger in
the land of Pandan-aram, and even after his return to
Canaan he had not dwelt continuously in one place. For
years, indeed, he had been at Hebron, near the Machpelah
cave, where the ashes of his father were entombed ; but
now again he was away from the only spots of earth in
Shechem and in Hebron which legally he could call his
own. So, with literal exactness, he could say that his life
had been a pilgrimage. But the expression had a forward
as well as a backward look. It told that he was seeking
a home beyond the grave, that he was desiring the better
country, " even the heavenly," and that his hopes were
anchored there. It indicated that his feelings regarding
his fathers were not so distinct and definite indeed, but of
the same kind as those of Baxter when he wrote concerning a venerable relative who died at the age of a hundred
years : " She has gone after many of my choicest friends,
and I am following even at the door. Had I been to enjoy
them only here, it would have been but a short comfort
mixed with many troubles which all our failings and sins,
and some degree of unsuitableness between the nearest
and dearest cause. But I am going after them, to that
blessed society where life and light and love, and therefore harmony, concord, and joy are perfect and everlasting." Thrice happy they who can look forward to
such an end of their Pilgrimage !

Then with what artless simplicity Jacob describes the character of his life—" Few and evil have the days of the years of my life been." Few? Yes, in the retrospect, the longest life appears but brief. " We spend our years as a tale that is told." Evil? Yes, for he had done much evil, and he had suffered much. They had not been only evil, for there were lines of light shot often through the gloom, but evil now preponderated in this view. " Alas ! for life, if this were all and naught beyond ! O earth ! " There is no answering the Psalmist's question, " Wherefore hast Thou made all men in vain ? " unless we take immortality into the account ; and if we did not believe in God, as the God and Father of the Lord Jesus Christ, and in the life and inmortality which our Saviour has brought to light, it would be hard to solve the question, " Is life worth living ? "   But take it as a pilgrimage to the better land beyond, and the journey will be held as more than compensated by the destination. Take it as a voyage " to the land immortal, the beautiful of lands," and the hardships of the passage will be as nothing compared with the glory to which it bears us, for

> When the shore is won at last
> Who will count the billows past ?

But now we must once more break off the interesting narrative, to gather up two or three valuable lessons.

We may learn, then, that in changing our residence, and going from one place to another, it is of the last importance that we secure that God shall go with us. One cannot read these chapters without thinking of the experiences of those who emigrate from the Old World to America, and of those who remove from the East to the new settlements in the far West. How often it is almost literally repeated ! First there comes one of the sons of the household ; it may be, forced to leave his home by the envies and jealousies of those

around him.   On his arrival he has difficulties to contend
with, and he has many alternations of fortune. Sometimes
he is as prosperous apparently as Joseph was in the house
of Potiphar, and sometimes almost as far down as Joseph
was when he was in prison.   But at length he finds his
sphere, and makes such good use of his opportunities that
he attains to competence and comfort, even, it may be, to
affluence.   Then he sends for his parents, and the tie
to the living, more strong than that to the dead, brings
them across to enjoy in their latest days the tender
nourishing of their long absent boy.   Or again, it is in the
far West, whither the young adventurer goes out to make
his way in the world.   He has had to endure many hardships, much that is little better than drudgery, and much
that makes him often sigh for the home which he has left.
But prosperity comes at last, and it will be robbed of half
its joy to him if his parents cannot share it with him.   So
at his bidding they arise and go.   Thus history repeats
itself, and this old story fits into multitudinous modern
instances.   But not always is sufficient heed given to the
sacrificing at Beersheba; and the point I make now is,
that in all such changes we should seek, above all things
else, the companionship of God.   Nothing will harm us
anywhere if God is with us, and we cannot have the
highest good if we go even into the fairest Goshen on
any continent without Him.

Horace Greeley, long ago, set the fashion of saying,
" Go West, young man, go West"; and there is wisdom
in the advice, " But don't go without your God."
Perhaps some are meditating on the propriety of their
pushing away into the places where the labour market
is not overstocked, and the opportunities are far better
than they are in a comparatively crowded city.   Nor
do we say a word against the project.   Go, by all
means, if you are not afraid to work; but remember

the sacrifice at Beersheba, and don't go without your God. Too many have done that, and have gone to ruin. But take Him with you, and He will be " your shield and your exceeding great reward."

But learn from this narrative never to be ashamed of any honest calling. Joseph's brothers were to tell Pharaoh frankly that they were shepherds, and that led to their settlement in Goshen. So, if you can work at a good trade, never think such handicraft beneath you. Paul was a tent-maker, and a greater than Paul wrought at the carpenter's bench in Nazareth. I emphasize this, because in these days there is a growing disposition among many to look down on trades and tradesmen. There is a spirit of cast among us, as really as there was in Egypt. Every kind of handicraft is regarded by many as menial, and when you call a thing by that name men and women flee from it as from a pestilence.

A young woman will reject comfort and safety in the situation of a domestic assistant, and long for a place in a public store, because the one is menial and the other not. And so many evils are created among us. A young man with marked mechanical ability will not go into the machine-shop because that makes him a workman, but he wants to go into an office or a store because that makes him a clerk—for " every tradesman is an abomination to our modern exquisites." Hence good, honest, skilled artisans are hard to get, and so we have too much bad workmanship. Hence, too, the supply of clerks is far ahead of the demand ; many are not employed at all, and those who are do not receive anything like an adequate salary, because their places can be supplied any day by others who will take less than they are receiving. It was a wise law among the Jews that every boy should learn a trade. He might follow it afterwards, or not, as he chose, but he had to learn one. It would be impracticable to

have any such law here; but I know that much misery
would be prevented, and great good accomplished if there
were less caste among us in this matter of handicraft, and
young men were more willing to work at the bench or
at the forge.   There is no disgrace in honest labour; nay,
since Jesus lived at Nazareth it has become Divine.   Read
such a life as that of George Stephenson, or James
Nasmyth, or Ichabod Washburn, and see how the branch
of opulence springs often out of the trunk of the tree of a
common handicraft.   The labour may be common, but
show you that the labourer is uncommon, and remember
well that

> Honour and shame from no condition rise;
> Act well your part—there all the honour lies.

Finally, remember that life at the longest is very short.
Therefore, do at once that which you feel you ought to do
at all.   Yea, do first that which is most important.   Seek
first the kingdom of God and His righteousness.   Young
man, do not leave it to a future day, but do it now, that
all your life may be one of usefulness and enjoyment.
Man of middle-age, you have a vivid sense of the rapidity
with which your years have gone, but they will go just as
rapidly in the future as in the past, and you will be on
your death-bed before you know it; therefore, "what thy
hands find to do, do it with all thy might." Man of old-age,
you have to make haste, for you have no time to lose.
The ancient law said kindly as to the sale of an estate,
"according to the number of the years thou shalt diminish
the price"; the nearer they were to the Jubilee, the
cheaper were they to sell their land.   So the nearer you
come to the end of your days, you ought to hold earthly
things more loosely, and prize heavenly things more
highly.   When your business day is drawing to a close,
you hasten to finish your work, and sometimes you do
more in the last hour than in all that went before.   As

your paper becomes more filled you write more closely, to get all in that you want to say. And, in the same way, the older you grow, you should become the more earnest in the service of your God in Christ. And if you have not yet begun to serve Him, I beseech you to begin now! When Napoleon came on the field of Marengo, it was late in the afternoon, and he saw that the battle was really lost. But looking at the western sun, he said, " There is just time to recover the day!" and giving out his orders with that rapid energy for which, combined with quick perception of what an emergency needed, he was so remarkable he turned a defeat into a victory. So your sun is nearing its setting, but there is time, in the present opportunity, to " recover the day." Avail yourself of it, therefore, at once, lest your life should end in utter, blank, eternal failure.

XI.

JOSEPH'S TWO VISITS TO HIS AGED FATHER.

GENESIS xlvii. 27; xlviii. 22.

IT would be observed by those who closely followed us in our last chapter, that we made no mention whatever of the genealogical list of the family of Jacob which is given in connection with the migration of the patriarch from Canaan to Egypt.* We took that course deliberately, in order that nothing of a merely formal sort might come in to break the continuity of our narrative, and no discussion of a question of difficulty might divert our attention from the practical lessons which the history suggested. But as the list to which I have referred has been a favourite armoury whence antagonists have drawn weapons for attacking the truthfulness of the book of Genesis, and has been the occasion of much perplexity to many candid students of the Scriptures, it may be well to devote a little time now to its elucidation.

The first thing that strikes the careful reader of this table is, that it contains the names of some who were not born at the date when Jacob went down to the land of Goshen. Thus, to say nothing of Hezron and Hamul, the grandsons of Judah, there are ten sons of Benjamin in the list; now, as Benjamin was a comparatively young

---

* Gen. xlvi. 8-27.

man, somewhere between twenty and thirty, at the time
of his removal to Egypt, it is at least highly improbable
that he should have had so large a family at that early
age. These and other anomalies in the table, therefore,
compel us to seek for the principle of its construction;
and when we discover the purpose which it was designed
to serve, we have at once the key to its explanation.

In the after-history of the Hebrew nation we find that
it was divided into twelve tribes, and that the tribes were
ranged under different families. The tribes, of course,
took their names from the twelve sons of Jacob, with
the exception that Manasseh and Ephraim, the sons of
Joseph, were reckoned as heads of tribes, precisely as if
they had been the sons and not merely the grandsons of
Jacob. In each tribe, again, the families into which it
was divided took their names from the grandsons of
Jacob, and in some cases—that of the tribe of Asher, for
example—from those of his great-grandsons. Now the
object of this list is to give the names of the heads of the
tribes, and those of the subordinate families of each tribe
in the nation.

Hence it belongs to a date slightly later than that
of the removal to Egypt, and is inserted here as the
most convenient place for its preservation, although it
undoubtedly contains the names of some who were not
born at the time of the emigration from Canaan, and who
are here said to have gone down into Egypt, simply on
the principle that, to use the language of the author of the
Epistle to the Hebrews, " they were then in the loins of
their fathers." This may seem to some as if it were
merely a violent cutting of the knot, rather than a patient
untying of it; but, as one has said, " There is a marked
difference in certain respects between genealogical and
historical records, and particularly in the mode of clubbing
together parent and offspring, or of giving sway to some

regulating principle."* They were very often constructed on some artificial principle. We cannot read the table with which Matthew begins his gospel without remarking that there other things are made to bend to the securing of fourteen generations between each of the different landing-places in the document. Now, in the list more immediately before us, the principle of construction was to include all the heads of families in the different tribes, whether these were grandsons or great-grandsons of Jacob, and whether they were born in Egypt or not; for as one is an English citizen who is born of English parents anywhere, so these were Hebrews though they were born in Egypt. Dean Payne Smith has put the matter very clearly and succinctly in these sentences: "This document is one that would be of the highest importance to the Israelites, when taking possession of Canaan, being, as it were, their title-deed to the land. Accordingly we find that it is drawn up in legal manner, representing as sons some who were really grandsons, but who took as heads of families the place usually held by sons. We next find that it represents them all as born in Canaan, not in a natural sense, but as the rightful heirs of the country. Technically, every head of a family was born in Canaan, and thus the danger was obviated of an objection to the possession of this rank being accorded to one born in Egypt."†

But there are difficulties also as to the numbers. The classification is arranged under the headings of Jacob's wives; and it is said, verse fifteenth, " These be the sons of Leah, which she bare unto Jacob in Padan-aram, with his daughter Dinah: all the souls of his sons and his

---

* Fairbairn's " Imperial Bible Dictionary," art. JACOB.
† Ellicott's "Old Testament Commentary for English Readers," vol. i. p. 159.

daughters were thirty-and-three." But when we add up the several items we get only thirty-two. This set us to a closer inspection of the wording of the document, and looking back to verse eighth we find, "These are the names of the children of Israel, which came into Egypt, Jacob and his sons." So, however strange it may seem, we must include Jacob himself in the enumeration, and that makes thirty-three.

Again, in the twenty-sixth verse, it is said, "All the souls that came with Jacob into Egypt, which came out of his loins, besides Jacob's sons' wives, all the souls were threescore and six; and the sons of Joseph, which were born him in Egypt, were two souls: all the souls of the house of Jacob, which came into Egypt, were threescore and ten." Now, how shall we explain these statements? If we add the totals for the sons of Leah, Rachel, Zilpah, and Bilhah as they are here given, we get the sum of seventy. But how shall we make out that of sixty-six? Thus: drop the name of Jacob from the sons of Leah and you have, including Dinah, thirty-two. Drop also Joseph and his two sons from the list of Rachel's descendants and you have for them eleven. This will give $32+16+11+7=66$. Then, if to these sixty-six thus accounted for you add Jacob, Joseph, and his two sons—four —you have seventy, the second number specified.

But some of you may remember that Stephen, in his address before the Jewish council, spoke thus: "Then sent Joseph and called his father Jacob to him, and all his kindred, threescore and fifteen souls." How now shall we explain that discrepancy? Some have accounted for it by supposing that Stephen quoted from the Septuagint, which includes in its genealogical list five descendants of Joseph who are not mentioned in the Hebrew text; while others have held that the eloquent deacon proceeded on the principle of excluding from the list all who were not

actually born in Canaan, and including the eleven wives
of Jacob's sons. Thus Dr. Lee, in his "Lectures on Inspiration," says, " Moses tells us how many Jacob and his
seed amounted to, omitting his sons' wives. Stephen
tells us how many they were that Joseph called into
Egypt. Some, therefore, in the list of Moses must be left
out of the number given by Stephen. Joseph and his two
sons could not be said to be called into Egypt, still less
could Hezron and Hamul, the sons of Pharez, who were
not yet born. Besides, Jacob, too, must be considered
apart. Hence six persons are to be deducted from the
number of Moses, in order to find those who are reckoned
by Stephen, and sixty-four only are common to both. Add
now the eleven wives of the sons of Jacob, and we get the
number, seventy-five, given by Stephen."* This seems
plausible, but the plausibility disappears when we go a
little into detail; for if we must deduct Hezron and
Hamul as not then born, plainly we must deduct, for the
same reason, some of the sons of Benjamin, and probably
also the grandsons of Asher; so that, in spite of its in-
genuity, this explanation of Dr. Lee's must be given up,
and we fall back on the other as entirely natural and
satisfactory, namely, that Stephen, speaking to Hellenistic
Jews, was quoting from the Greek version of the Old
Testament current in his day, which included five
descendants of Joseph, to wit, three grandsons and two
great-grandsons, who are not spoken of in the Hebrew
text, and only the sticklers for a mechanical and utterly
untenable theory of inspiration will be troubled by such
an explanation.

But, leaving now these matters of detail and difficulty,
let us take up the thread of the history at the point at
which we left it in our last chapter. Jacob resided in the

---

* " Donellan Lectures on Inspiration," p. 454.

land of Goshen for seventeen years, and as he removed from Canaan to Egypt in the second year of the great famine, he must have seen the land in its usual productiveness for twelve years. How it fared with Joseph all that while the narrative does not inform us, but there seems to be little doubt that he retained his exalted position in the country, even though the immediate occasion for his special services had passed away. He was still a great lord in the land, and his kinsmen were sharers in his prosperity, and continued to dwell in the district of Goshen. Only three incidents belonging to these seventeen years are recorded, and all of them cluster about the close of Jacob's life; but, whatever else may have marked the tenor of this last seventh portion of the pilgrimage of the aged patriarch—the Sabbath of his life, as we may call it—we may be sure that it was brightened for him by the fellowship, and lightened for him by the kindness of his beloved Joseph. Indeed, two out of the three incidents to which I have referred both illustrate and confirm that assertion.

The first was an interview between Jacob and Joseph themselves alone. The old man felt that his days on earth were drawing to a close. The frailties of age were upon him. He does not appear, indeed, to have been confined constantly to his couch, but his thoughts were much on his departure, and, in the course of nature, he knew that he must soon be "gathered to his fathers." But he saw no indication of the immediate return of his family to Canaan. Joseph most evidently had still work to do in Egypt, and Jacob's other sons were too comfortable under the shield of their brother's protection to desire to go elsewhere. As far, therefore, as he could forecast, Jacob felt that he should die in Egypt, and he began to ponder on the effect which that event would have upon the faith and character of his descendants. If he were to be buried in that land without giving any testimony to God's covenant, which had pledged

Jehovah to grant Canaan to his posterity, it would seem
like throwing up his claim to the Land of Promise altogether, and might reconcile his descendants to remain
for ever where they then were. But from that Jacob
revolted with all his heart. Accordingly, he sent specially
for Joseph, on whose truth and loyalty he could implicitly
depend, and required him to promise, with an oath
administered after the fashion of his fathers, that his
remains should not be buried in Egypt, but should be laid
in the Cave of Machpelah, beside those of Abraham and
Sarah, Isaac and Rebekah, and his own Leah.

This request was thus rooted in something deeper than
the merely natural desire of a man to have his body laid
beside those of his nearest kindred. Under the New
Testament dispensation, indeed, we have learned that it
makes no matter where our bodies are buried, for by His
brief occupancy of the tomb of Joseph the Lord Jesus
Christ has consecrated the whole earth as a cemetery for
His people ; and by His resurrection from the grave He has
given us the assurance that they that sleep in Him,
wheresoever their resting-places are, shall hear His voice
at the last great day, and shall come forth in spiritual and
incorruptible forms to meet Him in the skies. The mere
locality of our grave, therefore, is of comparatively small
importance, whether we are laid away under the arctic
snows, like the brave explorers who accompanied the
dauntless Franklin, or beneath the shade of tropical
shrubs on the rim of the Dark Continent, like those
missionary martyrs who, by their sepulchres, have taken
possession of the Machpelah in that new Land of Promise,
or in the dark, unfathomed caves of ocean, with the white
foam of the waves for our shroud, and the whistling of the
winds for our requiem. It is all one to the Christian
where his body is laid. And yet even the Christian has
the natural desire to be laid beside his kindred ; so that

in all our cemeteries we have family lots, and in many of
our old country homesteads we come yet upon the quiet
and secluded enclosure where the ashes of the first settlers
and those of their successors lie. But Jacob's desire that
his body should be laid in Machpelah had a deeper root
than nature. The land of Canaan was his by God's
covenant. He had not yet obtained it. For aught that
he could see, he was to die without entering on its
possession; but even in his death he would show that he
still believed that his children would have its ownership,
and therefore he made Joseph swear that he would bury
him in the sepulchre of his fathers.

Nor was this all. He wanted his sons and his decend-
ants to know that Egypt was not their rest. He desired
to fix their minds on Canaan, and to fan in their hearts
the desire to return thither when God should open up the
way. There was to be nothing, as far as he was concerned,
to anchor them in Egypt, but everything to incite them to
go back to Palestine; therefore, knowing how much there
is in the sepulchres of our fathers to gather round them
interest and enthusiasm, and to evoke the desire on our
part to be in their immediate neighbourhood, he said to
Joseph, " Bury me in the burying-place of my fathers."

Joseph took the required oath, saying, " I will do as thou
hast said "; and thereupon the anxiety of his father was
entirely removed. And we read that " Israel bowed
himself upon the bed's head." But the Septuagint
translation gives the phrase thus, " Israel bowed himself,
or worshipped, upon the top of his staff "; and the author
of the Epistle to the Hebrews quotes it, according to our
Authorised Version, thus, " Jacob worshipped, leaning
upon the top of his staff." It may appear strange that
two such diverse translations should be given of the same
Hebrew word, but an illustration will make it plain.
Originally the Hebrew was written without vowels, and these

were supplied by the reader. Latterly, however, and indeed centuries after the Christian era began, the Masoretes supplied the vowels, putting them in the shape of points under and in the consonants, very much as they are put in our modern phonographic short-hand. The same consonants, therefore, according as they were differently vowelled, might mean different things; just as in our own language the same consonants written in short-hand will signify trouble, or terrible, or treble, according as they are pointed. So here the same word in Hebrew vowelled one way means bed, and vowelled another means staff; and as the Greek translators were nearer the era when Hebrew was a spoken language, we prefer their rendering as the better.

But even with that translation, what is the meaning of the clause?   It has been commonly interpreted as a manifestation of Jacob's thankfulness to God for the ready acquiescence of Joseph in his request, and thus understood it harmonises well with the whole surroundings of the story and with all that we know of Jacob's own character. But Mr. Stuart Poole, in an article in the *Contemporary Review* for March, 1879, already referred to by me (see page 42), has suggested another, and perhaps a better explanation. He says, speaking of the conformity of the narrative of Joseph to the Egypt of the time as revealed by the monuments : " Two circumstances bring us very near Egyptian official usages. ' By the life of Pharaoh ' is used as a strong asseveration by Joseph ;* and when he has sworn to his father, after the Hebrew manner, that he will not bury him in Egypt, then Israel ' bowed himself upon the head of his staff.' " Both the expression " by the life of Pharaoh " and the custom of bowing upon the staff of an officer are traced by M.

---

* Genesis xliii. 15, 16.

Chabas, in his interesting essays on Egyptian judicial proceedings, where he cites the following passage describing
the taking of an oath by a witness in Thebes: "'He made
a life of the royal lord, striking his nose and his ears, and
placing himself on the head of the staff'—the ordinary
oath when the witness bowed himself on the magistrate's
staff of office." He well remarks that this explains the
passage in Genesis quoted above, as a recognition by
Jacob of his son's authority. According to this interesting
interpretation, then, the staff here is not that of Jacob,
but the official staff of Joseph, and Jacob shows his
gratitude to his son by rendering to him, after the
Egyptian manner, the respect which he was accustomed
to receive from the subjects of Pharaoh. This, too, is
a simple, natural, and every way appropriate exercise for
Jacob in the circumstances; and if I must choose between
the two explanations, I express my preference for the
second, as harmonising the Hebrew with the Septuagint,
the Old Testament with the New, and both with the
common custom of ancient Egypt.

The second incident which is recorded as having
occurred shortly before the death of Jacob is an interview between him and Joseph, in the presence of Ephraim
and Manasseh, and having special reference to them. In
response to a message telling him that his father was sick,
Joseph, accompanied by his two sons, hastened to Jacob's
bedside. When the old man heard of his approach he
summoned all his strength, and, rising to a sitting posture,
prepared himself for the discharge of an important duty.
After the usual greeting, of which here we have no account,
the venerable patriarch, looking far back in his history to
God's two appearances to him at Bethel, repeated to
Joseph the substance of the promises which the Lord had
there made to him, and formally adopted Ephraim and
Manasseh as his own sons, putting them, so far as tribal

prominence was concerned, on an equality with Joseph's
own brethren. Thus he spoke: "Now thy two sons,
Ephraim and Manasseh, which were born unto thee in
the land of Egypt, before I came unto thee into Egypt,
are mine; as Reuben and Simeon, they shall be mine.
And thy issue, which thou begettest after them, shall be
thine, and shall be called after the name of their brethren
in their inheritance." Then there comes into the narrative
a touch of nature which is exceedingly affecting. He has
been putting Ephraim and Manasseh into the birthright
place forfeited by Reuben, because to them, as the sons of
Joseph who was the first-born of Rachel, after its forfeiture by the first-born of Leah, it rightfully belonged;
and that suggests to him his first, his early, his constant,
his supreme love for Rachel, so that he goes on to speak
of her—of the time, place, and manner of her death, and
of her lonely grave, precisely as if the incidents had
happened only a short while before. It is *so* like an old
man in the apparent abruptness of the transition from his
grandsons to Rachel, and in the fond circumstantiality of
his references to his well-beloved; and those who have
had most to do with the aged will be the first to recognise
the truthful naturalness of the whole description.

But now, for the first time, the dying man, whose eyes
were dimmed with years, perceived that Joseph was not
alone. There were two others with him, but he could not
clearly identify them, and he asked, "Who are these?"
This led to Joseph's introduction of his sons to their
grandfather, who instantly said, "Bring them, I pray thee,
to me, and I will bless them"; and when he had kissed
and embraced them he said to their father, in a paren-
thesis of grateful love, "I had not thought to see thy face:
and, lo, God hath shewed me also thy seed." Then, when
they were kneeling before him, Manasseh, the elder, on the
left, where Jacob's right hand would come most naturally

to his head, and Ephraim, the younger, on the right,
where Jacob's left hand would most naturally find his
head, the old man crossed his hands, so that his right hand
was on the head of Ephraim and his left on that of
Manasseh, and in this attitude he repeated these beautiful
words : " God, before whom my fathers Abraham and
Isaac did walk, the God which fed me all my life long
unto this day, the Angel which redeemed me from all evil,
bless the lads ; and let my name be named on them, and
the name of my fathers Abraham and Isaac ; and let them
grow into a multitude in the midst of the earth." It was
the experience of a lifetime condensed into a sentence and
breathed into a prayer. The home of Beersheba, the
vision of Bethel, the protection experienced in Padan-
aram, the blessing of the new name from the angel that
wrestled with him at Peniel—all are brought into review
before us as we hear these words, and it seems as if all
were said that could be said by Jacob when he exclaimed,
"The Angel which redeemed me"—no created angel that,
but the only-beggotten Son who has redeemed us also, so
that across the chasm of milleniums our hands meet those
of Jacob, as we cling to Christ, and hear him saying,
"the Angel which redeemed me from all evil, bless the
lads."

But Joseph was slightly discomposed by the position of
his father's hands. He recognised that, like Isaac in
similar circumstances, Jacob was speaking under special
Divine guidance, and he would make sure that there was
no mistake. So he drew his father's attention to what he
had done, and received for answer, " I know it, my son, I
know it," with which he was content ; for to both the boys
Jacob had spoken as representing their descendants, in
words which truthfully describe the relative position of
the tribes of Ephraim and Manasseh in after days to each
other and to the rest of the nation.

Then, this interesting duty done, Jacob said to his son, "Behold, I die; but God shall be with you, and bring you again unto the land of your fathers"; and to give him yet another proof of the firmness of his faith in the Divine promise, he added, "Moreover, I have given to thee one portion above thy brethren, which I took out of the hand of the Amorite with my sword and with my bow." The word he rendered "portion" is "Shechem," and that, together with the declaration of the fourth Evangelist, that Jocob's well was "near to the parcel of ground which Jacob gave to his son Joseph," fixes the locality near the modern Nâblus, in that valley which is described by modern travellers as being the most beautiful place in all Palestine. But when did Jacob take that out of the hands of the Amorite with his sword and with his bow? Some have replied that it was when Simeon and Levi treacherously warred with the men of Shechem; but that can hardly be, for Jacob was grievously ashamed of their conduct, and emphatically condemned it, so that here he cannot be understood as appropriating and endorsing it. But there is no mention of any other strife with sword and bow in which Jacob was personally engaged, and therefore the common opinion now is, that he here spoke prophetically, and already saw the time in vision when his tribal descendants should conquer the Land of Promise, and Joseph's body should be laid in that portion of ground which, though it was his by inheritance, had to be taken again by Israel out of the hands of the Canaanites by force.

Thus far for the history. Now let us see what we can learn from it, that our exposition may be not merely for the satisfaction of the intellect, but also for the profit of the life. I mention only three things.

First, how delightful it is to see the intercourse between an aged father and a full-grown son, when it is what it ought to be on both sides. Joseph's greatest ambition

was to promote Jacob's welfare, and Jacob's heart rejoiced
in every honour which Joseph enjoyed. The Grand
Vizier of Egypt held himself at the proper call of his
father, but knowing how much he was engaged with
public and pressing affairs his father made demands
upon him only for necessary things. Joseph brought
Jacob to Egypt that he might nourish him, and he thought
it no hardship to have to provide for him as long as it was
necessary to do so; but Jacob, having brought his flocks
and herds with him, would not need such provision after
the famine ended, and would rejoice in his latest years
in a virtual independence. Joseph placed his father near
himself, that he might easily and often visit him; but
Jacob still kept up his own house, that he might not
interfere with the comfort of others, and they might not
mar the peace of his own heart. All this is very interesting, and not without its suggestive hints to us. It tells
those among us who have to provide for aged parents to
regard that as one of the highest honours of their lives.
An aged mother or a venerable father is the greatest
treasure that a son or a daughter can possess; and far
from counting their support a burden, their children
should regard it as a pleasure. But even where no
pecuniary support is needed by them, their sons ought
to go and see them often, and cheer them by their conversation and fellowship. The aged are lonely. They
have survived most of the companions of their youth
and middle age, and depend for many of their joys upon
those younger than themselves, especially upon their sons
and daughters. So go and see your father and mother
when you can; let nothing, if possible, keep you away
when they send for you, and when they are sick your
fitting place is by their bed. Sacredly cherish their
requests, and take upon you every responsibility that will
ease their hearts. They will not be with you long; and

when you lay their ashes in the dust, you will not be upbraided by the reproach of conscience that you did not honour and nourish them as you ought to have done.

But while in this fellowship there is an obligation resting on the son or daughter, there is a corresponding one devolving on the parent. He is to be considerate also of his son's or daughter's circumstances and duties, and is to remember that with advancing years on both sides the relative position of the one to the other has considerably changed. He cannot expect that he can be to his son or daughter as he was in the days of their minority, or that they can be to him precisely as they were when they were children ; and he must not murmur if other duties keep them from being with him as much as otherwise they would desire. The words of Lawson here are exceedingly judicious, and may be commended to the attentive consideration of those to whom they refer, " Children should obey and honour their parents as long as they live. But parents are not to expect the same degree of obedience from them in every part of life, because, in the progress of reason and of human affairs, children are entitled to new privileges, and laid under obligations to new duties. They have a right, when they come to the years of maturity, to judge for themselves concerning matters in which they were formerly bound to acquiesce in the judgment of their parents. They enter into new connections, the duties of which are not less sacred than those which they owed to their parents";* and nothing inconsistent with the performance of the duties of these relationships ought to be required even by their parents. These are valuable principles, and if

---

* " Lectures on the History of Joseph," by George Lawson, D.D., p. 390.

they were better understood among us there might be fewer family feuds or domestic misunderstandings.

Second, let us learn from this narrative that if we have any important business to transact before we die we should set about it betimes, and not leave it to be done in haste at the last. Jacob's end was drawing near, and he sent for Joseph, as it would appear, before even his last illness had set in, and ere yet he was laid upon his couch, to give him commandment concerning his burial. Now this may suggest, to those who have family arrangements to make, that they should not defer the making of them until they come to be in the article of death, but should settle their affairs while yet they are in full health, in the possession of a sound mind, and in calm, unbiassed spirit. If, for example, a will has to be made by a man—and every man, if he have anything to leave, both for his own sake and for the sake of those who are most nearly related to him, should make a will—why should he postpone the making of it until he come to die? It will not bring death any sooner if he should make it at once, and it may prevent many evils if it is made now. Then, if God should greatly prosper him in future years, and should thus alter his circumstances, let him destroy the former will and make another, lest terrible injustice and hardship be done to the survivors by putting them back into a scale of living to which they have not for long been accustomed, and leaving them with a pitiful provision instead of an ample sustenance such as could easily have been provided. I have known cases of great suffering just from this cause. Let every man keep his affairs well in hand, so that those around him shall have to mourn only his departure when he dies, and shall have no cause to blame him for want of thought for his nearest and his dearest relations. If there is anything that you feel you ought to do in the way of settling your affairs, so as to secure peace and comfort among the members of your family when you die, do it at once, for the uncertainty of life is proverbial, and you know not what a day may bring forth. You cannot read the newspapers for a week together without discovering that many unseemly squabbles over the division of property might have been prevented if those who in business were so energetic in the making of money had possessed only the foresight to arrange calmly, and in circumstances in which there could be no ground for the insinuation either of undue influence on the part of others or of incompetence on their own, for its division. If there is anything you feel impelled to say or do before you die, then say or do it now, and the older you are, let the *now* be only the more emphatic.

Finally, what a happy thing it is to have faith when we come to die. Jacob says, "*I die*, but *God* shall be with you." That was his legacy to Joseph and his other sons. He had no misgivings about them. They were in Egypt, no doubt, and he saw no present prospect of their return to Canaan, but he was sure that God would arrange all that, and he felt so confident about it that he gave commandment concerning his burial. He died away from the Land of Promise, but he " greeted it from afar," and on his death-bed re-affirmed his faith that his children would possess it. " God will be with you "; yes, and on the other side of it " he would be with God," in the true land of promise, the Canaan of the skies ; for that, as the author of the Epistle to the Hebrews assures us, was at the moment in his desire. But what was seen by him only through type becomes a direct object of faith to the Christian. Dying he leaves the Lord with his friends, and goes himself to be with the Lord. So he has calmness and peace like that which Michael Bruce has expressed in the beautiful hymn with which every Scotchman is familiar, as forming the last in the old Psalmody of his fatherland—

The hour of my departure's come,
I hear the voice that calls me home.
At last, O Lord, let trouble cease,
And let Thy servant die in peace.

The race appointed I have run ;
The combat's o'er, the prize is won ;
And now my witness is on high,
And now my record's in the sky.

Not in mine innocence I trust,
I bow before Thee in the dust ;
And through my Saviour's blood alone
I look for mercy at Thy throne.

I leave the world without a tear,
Save for the friends I held so dear ;
To heal their sorrows, Lord, descend,
And to the friendless prove a Friend.

Oh, for such faith in Christ through life, that we may
have this calmness and peace in the hour of our departure.

Amen.

XII.

JACOB'S DYING PROPHECIES.

GENESIS xlix. 1-27.

THE last of the three incidents in the life of Jacob which are recorded as having taken place between the migration of that patriarch to Egypt and his death, is the assembling by him of his sons around his death-bed, that he might tell them what should befall their posterity in the later days. It is commonly spoken of as his " blessing " of his children, but it would be more accurately described as his prophetic forecast of the future character, position, and history of each of the tribes which were to be named after each of his sons. The aged patriarch speaks throughout as one gifted for the occasion with Divine inspiration. His words are not mere wishes, nor are they simple prayers ; but they are actual predictions. He addresses his sons not merely as one who could say like the Highland chieftain—

'Tis the sunset of life gives me mystical lore,
And coming events cast their shadows before. *

but as the heir of the covenant blessing to whom a special revelation had been made, and who had received along with that the inspiration which was needed for its correct transmission to those for whom it was intended. Accordingly, by such as deny the possibility of prophecy, it has been industriously asserted that these patriarchal predic-

---

* Thomas Campbell.

tions must have been written after the occurrence of the things which they foretell, and that they are here fictitiously put into the mouth of Jacob. The very presence of such vaticinations in the document has been held by many as proving that it belongs to the date of David or of Solomon, and that it was written by one looking back upon the past, rather than spoken by one who was foretelling the future. Now it would be quite out of place to enter here on an elaborate reply to the *a priori* objection that prophecy is impossible, since that is only an inference from the assertion that all miracles are impossible, and such an assertion, as we have elsewhere shown,* amounts to a virtual denial of the personal existence of God Himself.

But in rebuttal of the affirmation that these predictions must have been written after the occurrence of the things which they foretell, we may point to the fact that in the portion which refers to Levi no mention is made of the consecration of the members of his tribe to the special service of God; and it is utterly inconceivable that one writing at any date subsequent to the erection of the Tabernacle should have passed that peculiar office of the Levites in silence. This prophecy, therefore, must have been given before the Exodus, and if that be so, no more fitting occasion for its enunciation can be suggested than that on which it is here said to have been uttered. Again, in the oracle which is addressed to Judah, there is, as we shall presently see, a reference to the time of the appearance of the Messiah on the earth; and even if the date of its production be put as far down as David's day, nothing would be gained in the interests of rationalism by that, since a difference of a few hundred years in the date of

---

* See " The Gospel Miracles in their relation to Christ and Christianity," by W. M. Taylor, D.D.   Lecture I.

a prediction, which is still acknowledged to be a thousand
years in advance of what we shall show to have been its
fulfilment, does not at all invalidate the supernatural
character of the prophecy. We take this chapter, therefore, as we find it, and we regard it as being what it pur-
ports to be, the dying utterance of the last of the three
great patriarchs.

Now, in carefully considering the separate oracles of
which it consists, we find two things specially characteristic of the whole series. In the first place, the tribes are
regarded as individuals, and the future of each is indicated
in an address to its head. Just as, among ourselves, a
nation is often viewed as a person, and its history as a
lifetime, having its birth, infancy, youth, manhood, old
age, and death, so each tribe here is personified in, or represented by, its progenitor, and his life is spoken of as
continued or prolonged in the existence of his posterity.
In the second place, each prediction is rooted in the
character or name of the individual addressed, and is
shown to be a development of some germ which had
already manifested its existence in him. In the vegetable
and animal kingdoms we find fixity of type maintained by
different species through long series of years, and the same
thing may be observed in the several tribes of men. Here
and there we may come upon individual exceptions, but
in the main the principle of heredity holds good, and the
descendants of the same progenitor have the qualities of
their sire. The Gauls of modern times have many of the
same characteristics which Paul attributes to the
Galatians of old, and they both come from the same stock.
Hence, Jacob here unconsciously proceeds on what is now
recognised as a law of nature, while at the same time his
allusions to the individual characters and actions of his
sons as they stood round his bed must have had a
particularly wholesome effect upon themselves, leading

some of them to the deepest penitence, and stimulating others to the devoutest praise.

We attempt no description of the scene. That which is not depicted is often, thereby, only the more effectively delineated. We leave you, therefore, to imagine the picture for yourselves, while we go on to give, in the briefest form, a clear presentation of the meaning of the different oracles. Jacob begins with Reuben, whom he thus addresses :—

> Reuben, my firstborn, thou,
> My might, and the beginning of my strength ;
> The excellency of dignity, and the excellency of power.
> Boiling over like water, thou shalt not excel ;
> Because thou wentest up to thy father's bed :
> Then defiledst thou it : he went up to my couch.

Here there is a reference to the forfeiture of the birthright by Reuben, and the sin of which that was the punishment. Its commission is traced to the geyser-like quality of Reuben's character, which burst forth intermittently, now boiling up in a sudden surge, and now receding out of sight. Of this peculiarity we have instances in his spasmodic and therefore unsuccessful attempt to save the life of Joseph by getting him put into the pit, and then leaving him, and in his altogether extravagant offer to allow his two sons to be slain if he did not bring Benjamin safely back. Now, such a temperament never achieves excellence. It lacks perseverance and steadiness of application, and Jacob affirms that Reuben's posterity, taking after their father in this respect, would never rise to any eminence in the nation. Nor did they ; for it is remarkable that no one of the Judges belonged to this tribe. It gave no great captain to the armies of Israel, and no name to the goodly fellowship of the prophets in the land. In the song of Deborah it is mentioned with disapprobation among those who

came not up to the help of the Lord ; and the unreliable-
ness of its members may be referred to in the words, " For
the divisions of Reuben there were great thoughts of
heart. Why abodest thou among the sheepfolds to hear
the bleatings of the flocks ? For the divisions of Reuben
there were great searchings of heart." So it passes down
into the region that is below mediocrity, and becomes the
tpye of superficial and short-lived impulse that dies away
into inactivity and inefficiency.

Simeon and Levi come next. They are addressed
together as having been the actors in that attack upon the
Shechemites which overwhelmed Jacob with shame, and
to which there is unmistakable allusion in these scorching
words :

> Simeon and Levi are brethren ;
> Instruments of cruelty are their swords.
> O my soul, come not thou into their secret ;
> Unto their assembly, mine honour, be not thou united ;
> For in their anger they slew a man,
> And in their selfwill they houghed oxen.
> Cursed be their anger, for it was fierce ;
> And their wrath, for it was cruel :
> I will divide them in Jacob,
> And scatter them in Israel.

They had conspired with each other for evil, and as a
punishment they would be scattered over the Land of
Promise. As Bishop Andrews has quaintly put it, " Their
fault was a bad union ; their punishment is a just division.
Their fault was ' hand-in-hand ' ; they were too near ; their
punishment is, they shall be set far enough asunder. So
whom the devil hath joined God puts insunder, and a
righteous thing it is it should be so." Now observe the
fulfilment. After the conquest of Canaan the Simeonites
were not important enough to have an allotment of their
own,* and had a portion out of the inheritance of Judah ;

---

* Joshua xix. 1-9.

and in the subsequent history of the nation it is difficult
to discover even the name of Simeon, or any trace of
influence exerted by the tribe.   Of the Levites we read
again and again that they had "no inheritance save God,"
and that their dwellings were assigned them in different
cities far from each other, and scattered over the territories
of all the tribes.   But there is this striking feature in their
case, namely, that what in Jacob's prophecy was a curse,
was turned, by the noble conduct of Moses and the splendid
loyalty of the Levites in a time of peril, into a blessing.
So that, while the letter of the prediction was fulfilled,
the penitence of the Levites had power, through the grace
of God, to change the spirit of it into a benediction.   The
truth of the prophecy was kept, but in the way of blessing
rather than of punishment; and few things are more
interesting and suggestive in this regard than the com-
parison of the words of Jacob concerning Levi with
the blessing which Moses pronounced upon the same
tribe.

Next comes Judah, to whom Jacob said—

> Judah, thou, thy brethren shall praise thee:
> Thy hand shall be on the neck of thine enemies;
> Thy father's children shall bow down before thee.
> Judah is a lion's whelp;
> From the prey, my son, thou art gone up:
> He stooped down, he crouched as a lion,
> And as an old lion; who shall rouse him up?
> A sceptre shall not depart from Judah,
> Nor a law-giver from between his feet,
> Until Shiloh come;
> And unto him shall be the obedience of the peoples.
> Binding his foal unto the vine,
> And his ass's colt unto the choice vine;
> He washed his garments in wine,
> And his clothes in the blood of grapes:
> His eyes shall be red with wine,
> And his teeth white with milk.

The first words of this oracle refer to the derivation of the name Judah, which signifies praise, and declare that he shall be the object of reverence among his brethren. The next verses depict his supremacy among the tribes as giving to them a king, and inaugurating a government which, in one form or other, should exist until the coming of Shiloh; while the closing verses describe the rich beauty and luxuriant productiveness of his tribal inheritance in the land of Canaan. But, naturally, we are most deeply interested in the portion which refers to the coming of Shiloh. Now here it is to be remarked that the translation which we have given is that which the majority of Hebrew scholars have sanctioned. The variation suggested by some, " until he come to Shiloh," finds little favour either on grammatical or historical grounds, and has been very generally discarded. The term Shiloh has been variously understood, but now the best scholars are divided between these two significations, "the Peaceful" and "He whose it is"—the one referring to the character of the Messiah, and the other to His right to the sceptre of Judah; but as the latter would require a considerable change in the Hebrew word, involving even the leaving out of one of its letters, I prefer the former, corresponding as it does with Isaiah's designation of the coming Deliverer as "the Prince of Peace." Now this prediction of Jacob is a distinct step forward in the march of prophecy. First, Messiah was to be the seed of the woman; then of the family of Shem, then of the seed of Abraham; then Jacob was designated as His progenitor, and now Judah. But along with that indication of His tribal ancestry we have now also this description of His character, the Peaceful, and this identification of the time of His appearance, namely, just before the sceptre shall depart from Judah. Now of these the first two need not detain us long, for " it is evident that our Lord sprang out

of Judah";* and every one recognises the fitness of
Shiloh, the Peaceful, as the name of Him on whose birth-
night the heavenly host sang "Glory to God in the
highest, peace on earth, good-will to men." But more
difficulty has been felt about the date, as here described,
and yet even here we have no need to shrink from the
strictest scrutiny. I cannot put the truth about it into
briefer or clearer sentences than the following, taken from
a valuable work : † "The figures used denote a continued
national existence on the part of Judah. . . . The sceptre
is emblematic of an actual executive authority, whether
king or magistrate, bearing sway over some definite
territory or country, rather than over a scattered race. . . .
The law-giver denotes that other indispensable adjunct to
a real nation, namely, the possession of its own legal
courts and institutions. [Now] over against this ancient
prophecy stands this fact in history, that, with the brief
exception of the stay in Babylon, . . . the tribe of Judah
maintained its specific existence from the beginning of
Hebrew history down to the overthrow by Titus, a nation
in the strict sense of the term where that is used in
distinction from a race or people." Under the Persians;
in the years of its independence after its successful conflict
with a portion of the empire left by Alexander ; and under
the Roman power, the Jewish nation preserved these
badges of its existence, and lost them only after that
memorable siege which Josephus has described, when
Jerusalem was destroyed and the people scattered over all
lands. Since then the Jews have been a race or people,
but not a nation, the sceptre has departed, the law-giver
has gone, because Shiloh has come ; and so in this

---

* Hebrews vii. 14.

† "The Great Argument," by W. H. Thomson, M.D., LL.D., pp. 104,
105.

prophecy, thus understood, we have a wonderful identification of Jesus of Nazareth as the true Messiah, for, as
the annotation on Genesis in the "Speakers' Commentary"
has said, " All Jewish antiquity referred this prophecy to
Messiah," and only since they have been pressed by the
argument that, if that be so, the time appointed for His
coming must have passed, have the Jews taken to in-
terpreting the passage of David and others.   Here,
therefore, we feel as formerly we did when expounding
the seventy sevens of Daniel.*   We survey an arch of
prophecy that spans eighteen hundred years, and as we
behold the correspondence between the event and the
prediction we ask who built that arch?   But if the Shiloh
has come, shall we not render to Him our obedience?
For the last clause of this verse is, " to Him shall
be the obedience of the peoples," that is, the nations
of the earth; and we have here the repetition in another
form of the promise to Abraham, that " in him and in
his seed all the nations of the earth should be blessed."
The Messiah was to be of the Jews, yet not for the
Jews alone, but for men as men; and the day is coming
when "all nations shall adore Him, and His praise all
people sing."

But we must hasten.   Zebulon comes next, and to him
Jacob says—

> Zebulon shall dwell at the haven of the sea;
> And he shall be for an haven of ships;
> And his border shall be towards Zidon.

This is a description of the tribal territory of Zebulon,
which stretched nearly, though not quite, across the
country from the Sea of Galilee in the east to the mari-
time plain of Phœnicia in the west, and which gave

---

* See " Daniel the Beloved," pp. 176-179.

the people not only a portion of very fertile land, but great facilities for trade and commerce with surrounding districts.

To Issachar, who follows next in order, the patriarch says—

> Issachar is a strong ass,
> Lying between the hurdles or sheepfolds;
> And he saw that rest was good,
> And the land that it was pleasant;
> And he bowed his shoulder to bear,
> And became a servant unto tribute."

This also refers to the position of the inheritance of the tribe of Issachar, which was one of the noblest in all Palestine, consisting as it did almost exactly of the plain of Esdraelon or Jezreel. Hence, as the years revolved, all that the people inhabiting that region wished was to be let alone. They had their joy and their reward in their daily work, and so, rather than be interrupted in that, they submitted to exactions by the marauding tribes who surrounded them, instead of manfully resisting their incursions and driving them away. They were too comfortable and I mphatic to withstand wrongs, and yet, when they were roused, they sent to the front good men and true— "men that had understanding of the times, who knew what Israel ought to do." * Not out of disrespect, therefore—for the ass was regarded as noble in the East in Jacob's day, and for long after—but as the best possible description of the character of his tribe, Issachar is portrayed as the big-boned, patient, strong, plodding ass, willingly submitting to the burden of tribute, if only he may have the present enjoyment of his good things—a type surviving still among us in the persons of those citizens who are too busy minding their own affairs to be

---

* 1 Chronicles xii. 32.

disturbed with public matters, and who will rather endure
injustice than put themselves to trouble in removing the
wrong-doers.

Following Issachar is Dan, the first of the sons of the
concubines on the list, and to him the patriarch exclaims—

> Dan shall judge his people,
> As one of the tribes of Israel.
> Dan shall be a serpent by the way, an adder in the path,
> That biteth the heels of the horse,
> So that his rider shall fall backward.

The meaning is that, though the son of Bilhah the concu-
bine, Dan should have a tribal existence and inheritance
equally with Reuben and the other sons of Leah, and that
in his warring with others he would manifest the qualities
of the serpent in the cunning of his attacks and the venom
of his bite.   Of this mode of assault we have illustrations
in the history of Samson, who belonged to this tribe, and
in the conduct of those colonists who robbed Micah of his
Levite and his gods, and went to wrest a settlement out of
the hands of the quiet and secure inhabitants of Laish.*
And the same qualities appear in those among the Mormons
who have either taken to themselves or been given the
name Danites, suggested, as some think, by this reference
to Dan as a serpent, and the connection of that animal
with the primal promise.

At this point in his address Jacob pauses a moment to
refresh his spirit by communion with his God, and gives
utterance to the pious ejaculation, " I have waited for Thy
salvation, O Lord "—as if he had said, " I have waited
long, but it is coming now. Soon shall I know Thy salvation
fully, and see Thy face in righteousness. The sooner the
better ; only give me strength to finish the work in which

---

* Judges xviii.

I am engaged." Then, thus refreshed in spirit, he resumed his prophetic utterances, and addressed Gad, saying—

> Gad, a troop shall overcome him:
> But he shall overcome at the last,

or, perhaps, "troops shall press on him, but he shall press upon their rear." There is here an allusion to the meaning of the word Gad, which signifies a troop,* and perhaps also to the exposed position of his territory on the east of Jordan, where he would be constantly open to attack by robbing tribes, who should often overcome him, but should also be harassed by him in return. A case of this kind is recorded in 1 Chron. v. 18-22, where the victory was given to the Gadites and their neighbours of Reuben and Manasseh, because "they cried to God in the battle, and He was entreated of them, because they had put their trust in Him."

Asher occupies the next place, and to him it is said—

> Out of Asher his bread shall be fat,
> And he shall yield royal dainties.

This refers to the fertility of the portion which fell to the lot of the tribe of Asher. That portion stretched along the coast of Sidonia, from Mount Carmel nearly to Mount Lebanon, and was specially rich in corn, wine, and oil. But there is no allusion to the character of the people, who seem to have had the indolence of those who dwell in a land that is spontaneously fertile, for they could not drive out the inhabitants of Achzib.† They gave no judge or warrior to Israel, and the only name which redeems the tribe from obscurity is that of the aged widow—Anna the prophetess—who received the infant Saviour in her arms,

---

* There is, besides, a humorous play on the words in the Hebrew, which is thus rendered by Bishop Browne: "Troops shall troop against him, but he shall troop on their retreat."

† Judges i. 31.

and of whom it is recorded that "she departed not from
the Temple at Jerusalem, but served God with prayers
and fastings night and day."

Naphtali is thus spoken of —

> Naphtali is a hind let loose:
> He giveth goodly words.

This has been variously explained.   Some have taken it as
meaning "Naphtali is a swift messenger, like a hind that
runneth on the mountains, bringing good tidings."   Others
regard it as describing a warrior of a free and independent
spirit, combining with his martial qualities those of poetry
and eloquence; and they find the verification of their
theory in the deeds of Barak and the song of Deborah,
since both of these worthies belonged to the tribe of
Naphtali.   Others see an allusion in the words to the
apostles who, "let loose" from Galilee, of which Naphtali's inheritance was a portion, brought to their fellow-
men the "good news" of salvation through Jesus Christ.
While still others, with an alteration merely of the vowel
points, make it read thus: "Naphtali is a spreading
terebinth-tree which puts forth goodly branches," and
refer it simply to the increase of the tribe.

And now we come to Joseph, and we shall find that,
although the venerable patriarch could not give to his
well-beloved son the coveted distinction of being the
progenitor of the Messiah, he yet laboured to heap up
blessings on his head, and showed even in this his latest
utterance that his early preference for his favourite son
remained with him to the end.   Its language is more
poetic than that of any of the other oracles, and its
length contrasts especially with the curt and hurried
brevity of those which immediately precede it, as if the
nearer the venerable speaker came to Joseph he was the
more impatient to reach him, and as if, when he had

reached him, he hardly knew how to tear himself away from blessing him. It is as follows—

Joseph is a fruitful bough,
A fruitful bough by a well;
Whose branches run over the wall :
The archers sorely grieved him,
They shot at him, and hated him :
But his bow abode in strength,
And the arms of his hands were made strong,
By the hands of the mighty *God* of Jacob ;
(From thence is the shepherd, the stone of Israel ;)
From the God of thy father, and He shall help thee,
And with the Almighty, even He shall bless thee with blessings of
heaven above,
Blessings of the deep that lieth under,
Blessings of the breasts, and of the womb.
The blessings of thy father prevail over the blessings of the **eternal**
mountains,
Even the glory of the everlasting hills ;
They shall be on the head of Joseph,
And on the crown of the head of him that was separate from his
brethren.

The first sentence of this oracle refers to the general prosperity of the house of Joseph, and the spreading of the branches of the tree over the wall may point to the fact that he alone of the twelve sons of Jacob was to be the progenitor of two tribes. The next verses may allude to the treatment of Joseph by his brethren and by Potiphar, and may take that as typical of the history of his tribes in after-days, and of the help which they were to receive of the Lord. In the phrase " from thence is the shepherd, the stone of Israel," some see a prophecy of Joshua, the great captain who came of the tribe of Ephraim, while others refer it to Joseph himself, and make it mean that he was so strengthened by God as to become " the shepherd of Israel," the sustainer of the whole of his family as well as of all Egypt in the time of famine and distress.

The blessings promised are in the main of a temporal sort. If we adhere to the Authorised Version of a passage which in the Hebrew is exceedingly obscure, these blessings were greater than those which Abraham and Isaac had pronounced upon their sons ; while if we follow the Septuagint, as we have done, the meaning is that the blessings of Joseph are greater than those of the mountains.   But in any case we hear a quiver in the old man's voice as, after this iteration and reiteration of benediction, he says, " Let them come on the head of Joseph and on the crown of the head of him who was separated from his brethren."

Last of all comes Benjamin, who is thus spoken of—

> Benjamin shall raven as a wolf:
> In the morning he shall devour the prey,
> And at night he shall divide the spoil.

The allusion in these words is clearly to the warlike character of the tribe of Benjamin, and, to borrow from an author already quoted in this chapter, "it is interesting in its indication of his restless and insatiable temperament. Although not a large tribe, as the wolf is less than the lion, yet ' little Benjamin ' made comparatively more mark in history than any of the others.   At one time, by a foolhardy but characteristic opposition to the united will of the nation, the Benjamites were nearly exterminated by their brethren.*   Subsequently to that, besides Ehud the Judge, Benjamin gave the first king to the nation in the person of Saul, whose heroic son, Jonathan, was a typical Benjamite.   The occurrence of men of this small tribe either as warriors, champions, or rebels, rendered it particularly famous for its hot blood and adventurous spirit, characteristics which, in the New Testament, found their highest exponent in the great Apostle, who was of

---

* Judges xix., xx., xxi.

the tribe of Benjamin, and who never rested or was satisfied in his labours." *

Thus far we have followed closely the utterances of the dying Jacob, and by doing so have left ourselves little time for anything in the way of practical application. But, in concluding, we may fall back upon three thoughts which have been already suggested in the course of our exposition, and may seek to give them greater prominence and force.

First, I would remind you of the different histories of the tribes of Simeon and Levi, as being alike fulfilments of one and the same prophecy. That was not because the prediction itself was, like some of the heathen oracles, so vague or so ambiguous that it could not be falsified by any event, for the phrases, " I will divide them in Jacob and scatter them in Israel," are both definite and clear. But the explanation is to be found in the subsequent conduct of the men of Levi, as contrasted with that of the men of Simeon, whereby in the one case the prophecy took the ultimate character of a blessing, and in the other it kept that of a curse. Now this was in the lifetime of a tribe which extended over hundreds of years, but something not dissimilar may occur in the lifetime of an individual. Let us suppose that two men have been guilty of the same sin, and that as the penal consequence they have both had to bear the same thing, namely, separation from their native land and virtual transportation to a new and strange country. But the one, unwarned thereby, continues in his wicked ways, and goes down and down in iniquity, until he ceases to be recognisable even by those who look for him; while the other, moved to penitence, begins a new career, earns an honourable independence, gives himself to public affairs, and becomes a benefactor to the colony or the state, so that at length his name is

---

* " The Great Argument," by W. H. Thomson, M.D., LL.D., p. 101.

everywhere mentioned with gratitude and respect. Here the proximate results in both cases were the same, but the ultimate how different! and all owing to the different dispositions of the two men. Nor is this an improbable supposition; you may have come on many cases like it, and they are full of warning to some and encouragement to others, not only for the present life, but also for that which is to come. Up to a certain point we have power, by our penitence, to make blessing for ourselves for the life that now is and for that which is to come; nay, even after we have lost the first opportunity, there may come another on a lower plane; but at length there is a limit, beyond which all such opportunities cease, and we must "dree our weird" eternally. Brethren and friends, we are all like Simeon and Levi, under one and the same condemnation —under a curse—but any one of us may, like Levi, through his penitence, turn the curse into a blessing, and become a priest of God; and if we do not, we must bear our own iniquity. Levi, after his penitence, became the teacher of the nation; and the sinner, after his restoration, may, just through his peculiar experience, be all the better fitted for helping other men. He can never be as he might have been if he had not sinned, but still his very sin may be so overruled that he may thereby acquire a special fitness for a special work. It all depends, however, upon his penitence. Therefore, let the sinner hearing me, whoever he may be, and whatever may have been the consequence of his sin, take heart and return to God in obedience and penitence rooted in and springing out of faith, and God may yet make out of him a Levite consecrated for some holy service.

Reverting again to the prophecy concerning Judah, how pleasant it is to observe that we have so many means of identifying the Messiah as the Sent of God! Any one prophecy clearly fulfilled would be enough, but we have the converging lines of almost all the predictions in the

Old Testament uniting ultimately in Him.   The very first one, which names Him as the seed of the woman, has in it such peculiar significance that we cannot help seeing at once its interpretation and fulfilment in the manner of His birth.   And in this utterance of Jacob, what could be more specific than His character as Shiloh, the Peaceful? or more definite than the date of His appearance before the close of the existence of the nation of the Jews?   But these are only specimens of all the rest.   " The testimony of Jesus is the spirit of prophecy."   Each of the ancient seers stands like another John the Baptist, pointing to the Messiah and saying, in his own distinctive way, in one form or another, " Behold the Lamb of God that taketh away the sin of the world."   I do not see how it is possible to resist the force of the argument which may be drawn to show that Christ, and Christ alone, meets and fulfils all the ancient oracles in the Old Testament Scriptures.   It proves that God was in the prophecies; it makes it clear that God was in the history, and it makes it certain that " God is in Christ."   Shall we not then receive Him, and rest upon Him, as our Redeemer? Shall we not submit to Him and obey Him as our Law-giver and King?   Shall not we, too, be among the peoples that " come bending before Him ? "

Finally, looking again at the characterisation of Issachar, we may see the enervating influence of too comfortable circumstances on a man or on a people.   The inheritance of Issachar was pleasant, fertile, easily cultivated, and exceedingly remunerative.   So his descendants came at length, for the most part, to take things easy, and sub-mitted to outrages which those in poorer circumstances must have resisted even to the death.   They grew indolent and luxurious, caring for little or nothing but their own ease, and sinking at last into mere tribute-payers.   Now all this reminds us of the truth that conflict is absolutely necessary to strength of character. He who has no difficulties to contend with has therein the great misfortune of his life; for he has little or no motive for exertion, and without exertion he will be nothing in particular. It is a serious affliction to a man to be too well off, and many a son has been ruined because he inherited a fortune from his father. Unvarying prosperity is not by any means an unmingled blessing, and may be often a great evil. In the struggle for existence which adversity causes many may sink, but the " survival " is always " of the fittest," for it is of those who have been made by the struggle into manly, earnest, strong, heroic souls. Do no plume yourself, therefore, on your easy circumstances, for they may make you only selfish, indolent, and lacking in public spirit, like that son of Jacob who had his fitting symbol in the contented, because well-fed and not over-loaded, ass.

But, on the other hand, do not whimper over your poverty, for, bravely wrestled with and nobly overcome, that may be the very making of you. Too much money has undone many a youth; too little has been the spur that has urged on many another to put forth all his strength, and so has developed and increased that strength. When you are getting comfortable and easy, therefore, suspect yourselves, and watch lest your patriotism should grow languid, your activity disappear, and self-sacrifice drop entirely out of your life. The mill-wheel stands still when there is too much water as well as when there is too little, and Agur's prayer is always safe—though not many offer it—" Give me neither poverty nor riches; feed me with food convenient for me: Lest I be full, and deny Thee, and say, Who is the Lord? or lest I be poor, and steal, and take the name of my God in vain." *

---

* Proverbs xxx. 8, 9.

XIII.

JACOB'S FUNERAL.

GENESIS xlix. 28; l. 14.

THE sons of Jacob were still around their father's
bed. His prophetic utterances had ceased, and
silence too sacred to be broken by any one of them had
settled down upon the group of brothers. Their father
was dying. They were with him on the very confines of
the other world, and their souls were hushed into solemnity.
It was no time for words of theirs, and so they waited
speechless for the end. But Jacob had not yet finished
his work. He had already, indeed, required Joseph to
promise with an oath that he would bury him in Canaan,
but there must be no unseemly dispute on such a matter
among them after he was gone, and therefore he gave to
them all the same charges concerning his funeral that he
had laid on Joseph, dwelling with affectionate detail on all
the particulars concerning Machpelah, and the loved ones
whose remains were laid within its cave. Then, having
" now nothing to do but to die," " he gathered up his feet
into the bed, and yielded up the ghost, and was gathered
unto his fathers."

This last expression is a historical reduplication of
Jacob's own words, for he had just before said, " I am to
be gathered unto my people," and it strikes the reader as
a little remarkable. It might, perhaps, be too much to
allege that there was in it, on Jacob's part, a recognition
of the immortality of the soul, and the communion of the
blessed in the disembodied state, and yet it does seem to
me to be something more than a mere euphemism for

death.   It is true, indeed, that the patriarch had not such
a clear revelation of the future life as Christ has now given
to us, and, therefore, we are not warranted to put into this
language, as it came from Jacob's lips, all that it would
imply in those of a dying Christian.   But still I cannot
help thinking that there was in it an expression of Jacob's
confidence that when he died he would consciously join
Isaac and Abraham in the fellowship of the immortals.
Somewhere these fathers of his were still in individual
spiritual existence, and thither death would take him to
share their happiness.   Thus, in parting from his sons his
comfort was that he himself was going to his fathers, to
enjoy with them nobler communion with their covenant
God than earth could ever afford.   They were in the
better Canaan, and he was about to join them there, so he
went in peace, like one who fell asleep.   And yet what a
change !   A little while ago and the intellect was bright
and clear, the voice was strong, and the mind all aglow
with a Divine inspiration which was bodying forth the
distinct description of the wondrous symbols under which
the future of the tribes had been revealed to him ; and now
there is nothing but a lifeless form, an empty house, whose
great inhabitant has gone.   It is a dreadful mystery ; one
moment the father speaks in love and tenderness, the next
you speak to him and he is not there, but has gone by a
door you have not seen into a realm so near that there is
but a thin veil between you and it, and yet so far that the
separation of a continent is not so thorough.

> Life and Thought have gone away
>   Side by side,
>   Leaving door and windows wide.
> Careless tenants they !
>
> All within is dark as night :
> In the windows is no light ;
> And no murmur at the door.
> So frequent on its hinge before.

Close the door, the shutters close,
Or thro' the windows we shall see
The nakedness and vacancy
Of the dark deserted house.*

So, perhaps, Joseph felt when he advanced, according to the promise that went before concerning him, and put his hand upon his father's eyes to shut their lids for the last time, and hide their soullessness from view. But he could not perform that office of affection without the deepest emotion, for, as he did it, all the past would come rushing back upon him, and give intensity to the pang of the present. The early love that clothed him in the costly robe combined with the later pride that rejoiced so unfeignedly in his Egyptian greatness to move him into tears. It was the first time since he knew its meaning that death had come so near himself. He was too young to realise all his loss when his mother Rachel had been taken. But now, after those seventeen years of unalloyed delight in each other, which they had been permitted to enjoy as the sequel to the varied experiences through which they had both been brought; after they had come really to know and appreciate each other in that endearing intercourse in which the fatherhood of the one and the sonship of the other had risen into the noblest sort of brotherhood, his father is laid low, and he feels the blow most keenly. True, Jacob was an old man, but, strange as it may seem to some, that only made him dearer, and, most of all, he was his *father* once before lost, and only recently restored; and the thought of that so overpowered him "that he fell upon his face, and wept upon him, and kissed him."

But even such grief as that must not hinder him from carrying out his father's commands, and so, as representing his brothers, he took upon himself all the arrangements

* Tennyson.

for the funeral. But while complying with the wish of his parent, he at the same time conformed, as far as it was possible or practicable, to the customs of the country with which he was himself so prominently identified. It will contribute, therefore, to a better understanding of the narrative, if we should give you here, as succinctly as possible, an account of the Egyptian manner of disposing of the dead. It was part of the creed of those ancient people that at death the soul of a man entered into the body of an animal, and passed from that through a series of such transmigrations until it was thoroughly purified, when it returned to that to which it had originally belonged. They believed thus in what was known among the Greeks as " metempsychosis," and also in the resumption of the body by the soul after the appointed circle of transmigrations had been finished. Their doctrine thus was not that of the resurrection of the body, as Paul teaches it, but rather that of the actual resumption by the soul of the identical body which it had left at first, and faith in that led them to take means for the preservation of the body " in order to keep it in a fit state to receive the soul which once inhabited it ; and the various occupations followed by the Egyptians during the lifetime of the deceased, which were represented in the sculptures, as well as his arms, the implements he used, or whatever was most precious to him, which were deposited in the tomb with his coffin, might be intended for his benefit at the time of his re-union, which at the least possible period was fixed at three thousand years." *   The process which they

---

* Wilkinson, " Ancient Egyptians," vol. iii. p. 465. But Wilkinson does not speak with absolute decision on this point, and the paragraph immediately following that from which the above extract is taken begins thus : " We are, therefore, still in uncertainty respecting the actual intentions of the Egyptians in thus preserving the body and ornamenting their sepulchres at so great expense ; nor is there any decided proof that

followed for this preservation of the body was that which we now know as embalming, and which has been minutely described by such ancient writers as Herodotus and Diodorus. There were three different methods, varying in the extent of the operations performed and in the amount of expense incurred. The most costly process, which was most likely that adopted in the case of Jacob, and which required an outlay of about two hundred and fifty pounds, consisted in the removal of the brain and the viscera, the washing of the cavities thus made with certain fragrant liquors, the filling of these with powder of myrrh, cassia, and other spices, and then the placing of the whole body thus prepared in a solution of natron—*i.e.*, saltpetre—for a certain specified number of days. * When these were fulfilled, the body was washed, and wrapped up in bands of fine linen, which were fastened on the inner side with gum, and which often

---

the resurrection of the body was a tenet of their religion. It is, however, highly probable that such was their belief, since no other satisfactory reason can be given for the great care of the body after death." For resurrection we should read resumption of the body, since the former term ought now to be restricted to such a passing on to a higher human life as Paul has described.

* It has, however, been doubted whether these ancient authors give all the secret of the embalming process. Thornley Smith has the following in a note in his volume on Joseph, p. 259: "It has been found that the process described by Herodotus and Diodorus is not effectual in preserving bodies long, so that it is supposed by some that there was a secret in the art with which they were not acquainted"; and a writer in the *Athenæum* for June, 1850, states it as his opinion: "(1) That an essential part of the mummifying process was the application of heat to the body, previously filled with tarry substances and securely wrapped in a dense layer of bandages; and (2) That of necessity in bodies so treated must be formed by the two (as a product of its decomposition by heat) that substance to which the name of creosote has been given, from its flesh-preserving properties (κρέως and σωτήρ), and which was first obtained as a separate substance by Reechenbach."

extended to the length of a thousand yards. After all this, which required forty days, the body was delivered over to the relatives, who placed it in a stone or wooden coffin; and then the proper family mourning began. That lasted for thirty days, and at the close of these came the funeral services, which are thus described by Wilkinson, who quotes mainly from Diodorus.

But before I give his statements, permit me to premise that every large city—such as Thebes, Memphis, and other places—had its sacred lake, on the farther shore of which were the tombs in which the cases or coffins containing the embalmed bodies were buried. When the tomb was ready, and all the necessary preparations had been made, "the coffin, or mummy-case, was carried forth and deposited in the hearse, drawn upon a sledge, to the sacred lake of the Nome" (department or district), notice having been previously given to the judges, and a public announcement made of the appointed day. Forty-two judges having been summoned and placed in a semicircle near the banks of the lake, a boat was brought up, provided expressly for the occasion, under the direction of a boatman, called in the Egyptian language Charon, and it is from hence that the fable is said to be derived which Orpheus introduced into Greece. For while in Egypt he had witnessed this ceremony, and he imitated a portion of it, and supplied the rest from his own imagination. When the boat was ready for the reception of the coffin, it was lawful for any person who thought proper to bring forward his accusation against the deceased. If it could be proved that he had led an evil life, the judges declared accordingly, and the body was deprived of the accustomed sepulture; but if the accuser failed to establish what he advanced, he was subject to the heaviest penalties. When there was no accuser, or when the accusation had been disproved, the relations ceased from their lamentations, and pronounced encomiums on the deceased. They did not enlarge upon his descent, as is usual among the Greeks—for they held that all the Egyptians are equally noble—but they related his early education and the course of his studies, and then, praising his piety and justice in manhood, his temperance, and the other virtues he possessed, they supplicated the gods below to receive him as a companion of the pious. This announcement was received by the assembled multitude with acclamations, and they joined in extolling the glory of the deceased, who was about to remain forever with the virtuous in the regions of Hades. The body was then taken by those who had family catacombs already prepared, and placed in the repository allotted to it."*

This description, abundantly interesting and deeply suggestive in itself, will enable us at once to see in how far Joseph observed, and in how far he deviated from, the customs of Egypt in arranging for the funeral of his father. We read that " he commanded his servants the physicians to embalm his father "—a statement which seems to our modern ears a little peculiar. But it has to be born in mind that in the Egypt of that day every physician confined himself to the study and treatment of one disease, or of the diseases of one organ of the body ; so that the medical men then were all what we should now call specialists, and a grandee like Joseph would require in his establishment a whole faculty of doctors.† It was thus the most natural thing in the world that the embalming arrangements should be put under the direction of these professional men, though the actual carrying of them out might be left to the class of persons who were known as embalmers, and who devoted themselves exclusively to that particular work. This filled up forty days. Then came the thirty days of

---

* Wilkinson's " The Ancient Egyptians," vol. iii. pp. 453, 454.

·† On this point see Wilkinson, vol. ii. pp. 355, 356 ; vol. iii. p. 477.

mourning, during which the custom of the Egyptians was, that "the family mourned at home, singing the funeral dirge, and all the time they abstained from the bath, wine, the delicacies of the table, and rich clothing. On the death in any house of a person of consequence, forthwith the women beplastered their heads, and sometimes even their faces, with mud, and sallied forth, wandering through the city with their dresses fastened with a band and their bosoms bare, beating themselves as they walked. The men, similarly begirt, beat their breasts separately."* Joseph, therefore, with his brethren, sat in seclusion, unshaven and unwashed; while without, in token of honour to his father for his sake, the people, after their own custom, would do as Herodotus, in the words I have just quoted, has described; for this was a public mourning, and the public arrangements, therefore, were not in Joseph's hands.

But now the time for the removing of the remains of his father to Canaan drew nigh. He could not do that, however, without the permission of Pharaoh, and in his mourning undress, unshaven and unwashed, he could not go personally to the monarch. Therefore he sought the mediation of others, and through those already in the house of Pharaoh he presented his request that he might be permitted to take Jacob's remains to Canaan, giving natural, and perhaps also politic, prominence to the fact that he was seeking to carry out a promise which, under solemn oath, he had made to his father. The permission asked was granted, and the twelve brothers and their families, with but the exception of the little ones, and accompanied by a goodly array of chariots and horsemen from among the Egyptians, set out from Goshen for the land of Canaan. We have no particulars about the route which they followed, nor can we certainly identify the

---

* Rawlinson's "Herodotus," as quoted by Jamieson. Comm. *in loco.*

threshing-floor of Atad, where they halted for seven days
for the completion of the mourning services, though there
is no trace of any such judgment ordeal as that which the
Egyptians held on the margin of their sacred lake. All
we know is that the lamentations were so great as to
attract the attention of the inhabitants, who named
the place always afterwards Abel-Mizraim—the field
or mourning of the Egyptians. It has not yet been
discovered, and there is some doubt about its site, but
taking the phrase, "which is beyond Jordan," as written
by one still on its eastern shore, we incline to the belief
that we are to look for Abel-Mizraim on the western side
of that river; and, perhaps, they may not be far out of the
way who put it in the neighbourhood of Hebron. At that
place, wherever it was, the children of the patriarch left
their Egyptian convoy for the time, while they took the
remains of their father and reverently laid them in the
Cave of Machpelah beside those of his kindred.

What an interesting place that Hebron cave must be!
Unlike many of the so-called sacred sites now pointed out
to travellers in Palestine, this one is authentic and undoubted. In the name of the city, El Khulil—the Friend
—there is a striking memorial of Abraham himself, "the
friend of God," and the field which he bought from
Ephron the Hittite is still identified. It is occupied now
by a great mosque, whose external wall forms a parallelo-
gram one hundred and ninety-eight feet long by one
hundred and thirteen and a-half broad. The height of the
wall is forty-eight feet, and the masonry of which it is
composed is so msssive as to recall to the traveller that of
the Temple walls at the Jew's wailing-place in Jerusalem.
Entrance into this mosque has been so sacredly guarded
that no one not a Mahomedan gained admission into it
for, I suppose, centuries, until the Prince of Wales,
accompanied by Dean Stanley, General Bruce, and

Dr. Rosen, were permitted to go in on the occasion
of the visit made by the Prince to Palestine in
1862. Since then a like privilege has been accorded to
Mr. Fergusson the architect, the Marquis of Bute, M.
Pierotti, and the Crown Prince of Prussia. Dean Stanley
has given a most interesting description, both of the
diplomatic means which were used for gaining admission
and of the interior of the mosque itself, in the appendix to
the first volume of his " Lectures on the History of the
Jewish Church," from which I take the following ex-
tracts : " With regard to the building itself, two points at
once became apparent. First, it was clear that it had
been originally a Byzantine church ; . . . second, it was
clear that it had been converted at a much later period
into a mosque. The tombs of the patriarchs do not
profess to be the actual places of sepulture, but are merely
monuments or cenotaphs in honour of the dead who lie
beneath. Each is enclosed within a separate chapel or
shrine, closed with gates or railings similar to those which
surround or enclose the special chapels or royal tombs in
Westminster Abbey. The two first of these are contained
in the inner portico or narthex before the entrance into
the actual building of the mosque. In the recess on the
right is the shrine of Abraham ; in the recess on the left
that of Sarah, each guarded by silver gates. The shrine of
Sarah we were requested not to enter, as being that of a
woman. . . . Within the area of the church or mosque
were shown the tombs of Isaac and Rebekah. They are
placed under separate chapels, in the walls of which are
windows, and of which the gates are grated, not with
silver, but iron bars. . . . The shrines of Jacob and
Leah were shown in recesses corresponding to those of
Abraham and Sarah, but in a separate cloister opposite
to the entrance of the mosque. Against Leah's tomb, as
seen through the iron grate, two green banners reclined,

the origin and meaning of which were unknown."
Another tomb shown is that of Joseph, who, however,
was buried at Shechem ; and on the outside of the
mosque are two shrines, which are said to be merely orna-
mental. The dean proceeds : " One indication alone of
the cavern beneath was visible. In the interior of the
mosque, at the corner of the shrine of Abraham, was a
small circular hole, about eight inches across, of which
one foot above the pavement was built of strong
masonry, but of which the lower part, as far as we could
see and feel, was of the living rock. This cavity appeared
to open into a dark space beneath, and that space (which
the guardians of the mosque believed to extend under the
whole platform) can hardly be anything else than the
ancient cavern of Machpelah. This was the only aperture which the guardians recognised. 'Once,' they said,
' two thousand five hundred years ago, a servant of a great
king had penetrated through some other entrance. He
descended in full possession of his faculties and of remarkable corpulence ; he returned blind, deaf, withered and
crippled.' Since then the entrance was closed, and this
aperture alone was left—partly for the sake of suffering
the holy air of the cave to escape into the mosque and be
scented by the faithful, partly for the sake of allowing a
lamp to be let down by a chain which we saw suspended
at the mouth, to burn upon the sacred grave. We asked
whether it could not be lighted now ? 'No,' they said ;
' the saint likes to have a lamp at night, but not in the full
daylight.' With that glimpse into the dark void we and
the world without must for the present be satisfied.
Whether any other entrance is known to the Mussulmans
themselves must be a matter of doubt. The original
entrance to the cave, if it is now to be found at all, must
probably be on the southern face of the hill, between the
mosque and the gallery containing the shrine of Joseph,

and entirely obstructed by the ancient Jewish wall probably built across it for this very purpose."* Such, up to the present date, is all that is known of Machpelah; but we may hope that, as Turkish power wanes in the East, and Mussulman exclusiveness gives way before the inevitable influence of the modern intercourse of nation with nation, the cave itself will be explored, and the veritable mummy of Jacob be exhumed to bear its irrefutable testimony of the truthfulness of this ancient history.

We read of no services at the place of burial, and we may not presume to conjecture what was said or done at the grave. All we know is that the twelve brothers left the remains of their venerable father there, and turned away, no doubt, in pensive mood, to go back to their children and their flocks, and their common occupations in the land of Goshen. All of us have experienced how hard a thing it is to take up the cares and work of our common lives, after their paltriness has been seen by us at the tomb of a beloved one, and without the solace and joy which we were wont to receive from his fellowship and encouragement. But yet it has to be done, and in the doing of it there is, in God's good Providence, a compensation of comfort; for every mourner will tell you that his consolation has come to him most richly when, looking up to God for support, he has set himself to the discharge of daily duty, and forgotten himself in the service of his master, in the sphere of his appointment.

But now, as we take leave of Jacob, we cannot but be reminded of the great lesson of his life. A strangely chequered career it was which ended in this great funeral at Machpelah; but it is clearly divided into two portions, both of which are alike instructive to the Bible student. In the outset we find in him little attractiveness. True,

---

* Stanley's " Jewish Church," vol. i. pp. 431-442.

even from the first, there must have been in him a winsome
affectionateness of disposition which gained for him his
mother's partiality. But he was by nature, then, as well
as by name, the supplanter, a master of intrigue, who once
and again outwitted his rough, blunt, and bold Bedouin
brother Esau. Yet withal, unscrupulous as he was, let us
not forget to note that from the first his eye was on the
future, and that he lived for that. Therein lay the great
difference between him and his brother. Esau cared for
nothing but the present. Give him the pleasures of the
chase, the gratification of appetite, and the enjoyment of
the moment, and he was content. But Jacob had the
consciousness that there was a future before him. He
knew that the mysterious birthright was to be his; to that
his mother had taught him always to look forward; and
though he had little idea then of all that was involved in
it, and had not enough faith in God to leave the time and
manner of his getting it entirely to Him, yet he did
subordinate to its attainment many things in the present.
Still, even to get that good, he did the evil of deceit, and
so, up to his departure from his father's house, we have
little genuine admiration for his character or conduct.
But with the Bethel vision his new life began. Then for
the first time he came face to face with God, and from
that hour the Divine training of the heir to the covenant
commenced. He was sent to Laban's house, that there,
from his own practical experience, he might learn what an
evil and a bitter thing it is to be deceived; and though
there remained, after all the discipline of these twenty
years, some of his old self-trusting subtlety, which led to
his stealthy flight, all that was ultimately dislodged from
him by the Peniel wrestling. He went over the Jabbok
that night to pray earnestly for placability towards him in
the heart of Esau, and there he was again confronted by
the covenant angel, who virtually said to him, " It is not

Esau that you have to fear. The greatest evil for you is the enmity of God, and if you can secure deliverance from that all else will soon be well. Right with God, you may trust Him to set you right with your brother." This led him to forget his first errand across the ford, so that, instead of crying for the appeasement of Esau, he exclaimed, " Tell me Thy name, Thou great unknown"; and with the revelation of that *Love* which is the nature and the name of God, there came to him, as with the same revelation there comes yet to every man, the new name and the new nature, Israel. Thenceforward he is all that we could desire him to be. His trials, indeed, continue ; for, as Wilberforce[*] remarks, " The punishment of the ' supplanter's ' subtlety lasted on after its sin had been forgiven to the Prince of God"; but through all these trials—the folly of Reuben, the dishonour of Dinah, the cruelty of Simeon and Levi, the deceit of his sons, the loss of Joseph—we see the chastened spirit of a saint, and in the end he goes down, like the sun in the summer sky, through banks of glory clouds, leaving a trail of radiant purple behind him that ravishes the eye of every beholder. Thus a career that began in deceit was closed in excellence.

Now, with such a history contrast that of a man, say, like King Saul. We are attracted to him from the very first. We do not wonder that the people, when they saw him[†] on his election-day, raised the glad shout, " Long live the king ! " We admire the promptitude, the energy, and the bravery of his conduct in his deliverance of the men of Jabesh Gilead ; and even after his sin in the matter of the Amalekites, we are not surprised that Samuel should have so clung to him and loved him ; indeed, we rather agree with the old prophet in the sentiment. But as his life course goes on, there is a constant

---

* " Heroes of Hebrew History," p. 51.   † 1 Samuel x. 24.

deterioration in his character. His envy of David comes out. His cruelty, his cunning, his vindictiveness make their appearance, and we follow him down and down and down until we find him at the door of the Endor cave, committing what one has described as "probably as nearly the sin against the Holy Ghost as it was possible for one under the old covenant, and before the day of Pentecost,* to commit." Here, therefore, there was just the opposite of that which we have seen in Jacob. Here was a career opening with splendid promise and with much attractiveness, but closed in utmost dishonour. And what we have marked in these two contrasted histories we may see—some of us, perhaps, have often seen—in the careers of modern men. Now how shall we explain the difference? Thus all Jacob's trials sent him to God, and shook him out of himself; all those of Saul drove him away from God, and rooted him more firmly in himself. And in that explanation lies the lesson of Jacob's life. No matter what your past career may have had in it of what was evil, supplanting, dishonourable, there is hope for you, if you will go to God and ask Him to reveal His name to you. There is a door-way in that out into a new and nobler self for you. But, on the other hand, no matter how much there has been of promise and apparent prophecy of good in your past career, it will surely end in blackest disappointment to you and all around you if you attempt to build your future simply on yourselves. Your relation to God will ultimately determine everything about you—of character and real success in life. If thus far you have failed, betake yourself to God in Christ, and that will be your Bethel, or Peniel, the turning-point of your history, the water-shed of your life. And again, whatever of loveliness

---

* Trench's "Shipwrecks of Faith," p. 45.

there may have been thus far about you, that is enduring only in as far as you connect it with God in Christ. Young men, take this lesson with you from the contrast between the Machpelah funeral of Jacob and the dark ending of that royal life on Mount Gilboa, and that it may have all the more power with you, let me give it in the words of Archbishop Trench: " Build on no good thing which you find within yourselves. Humane, generous, high-minded, brave you may be, cherishing large purposes for the welfare of others, willing to devote yourselves in a spirit of earnest self-sacrifice to their good. But life is strong—how strong none can guess till they have tried to abate the edge of high resolutions, to dwarf, to stunt, and at last to strangle the nobler growths of the soul, to lead men to forget, sometimes, alas! to despise the loftier dreams and purer aspirations of their youth. There is only one pledge for the permanence of any good thing that is in you, namely, that you bring it *to* God, and that you reserve it *for* God with that higher consecration which He only can give it—not now any more a virtue of this world, but a grace of the kingdom of heaven; and that you bring it to Him again and again, for indeed all your fresh springs must be in Him; and they that wait on Him, they, and they only, renew their strength, run and are not weary, walk and are not faint; they, and they only, bring forth fruit in old age to show that the Lord is upright, and that there is no unrighteousness in Him."*

---

* Trench's " Shipwrecks of Faith," pp. 55, 56.

XIV.

JOSEPH'S DEATH.

GENESIS l. 15-26.

FROM Machpelah the brothers returned to Egypt to resume their usual work. But the absence of Jacob re-awakened in the hearts of ten of them the sense of their ill-desert for their treatment of Joseph long ago, and made them fear that now he might visit them with the punishment which their cruelty had merited. They supposed that their brother's kindness to them had been shown simply for their father's sake, and that it was Jacob's presence alone that secured their immunity. They knew Joseph so imperfectly that they judged him to have a disposition like that of Esau, who threatened his brother after this fashion : " The days of mourning for my father are at hand ; then will I slay my brother Jacob " ;* and they were afraid lest now he should be moved, either to put them to death, or to subject them to some most ignominious treatment. But it was not the presence of Jacob that had moved Joseph to his clemency. Had that been all that held him from revenge they might well have trembled ; for he had the power of Egypt at his back, and there was no one in the kingdom who would have called him to account either for its use or its abuse. But that which weighed with Joseph was his experience of the nearness and the goodness of his God. Jacob might die,

---

* Genesis xxvii. 41.

but God remained, and that God had been with him and
made him prosperous in everything he did. It would
have been a poor return, therefore, for his goodness, if he
had dealt sternly and implacably with his own brothers.
His gratitude for the Divine favour thus showed itself in
his tenderness towards them after he was fully convinced
that they had truly acknowledged their guilt, and heartily
repented of their sin. He put them to a severe test, in
order to find out how they felt about their conduct towards
himself, but when once he was satisfied on that point he
frankly, fully, and permanently forgave them.

It is a hard thing to forgive those who have done us
grievous injury. We may, perhaps, without much difficulty come so far as to refrain from visiting them
with positive punishment. But to be to them as we
would have been if they had never wronged us; to have
no constraint in our intercourse with them from our
remembrance of their attempt to do us harm; to take
them back into our confidence again, and trust them as
if nothing had occurred—*that* is hard indeed. Yet, if we
are thoroughly persuaded of the genuineness of their
repentance, and have ourselves a deep sense of gratitude
to God for His remission of our own sins against Him,
we may be enabled by His grace and spirit to deal with
others as He has dealt with ourselves.

But hard as it is to forgive, it is a yet more difficult
thing for human nature, unaided by Divine grace, frankly
and unsuspectingly to accept forgiveness. The wrong-
doer measures others by himself, and therefore he is
always suspicious that there is some lurking treachery
in the overtures of reconciliation that are made to him
by the man whom he has injured. He cannot believe
in disinterested generosity or undesigning goodness, and
therefore he is apt to treat all offers of forgiveness as
snares which have been set in order the more effectually

to catch him for punishment. This is the reason why men so generally reject the message of the Gospel itself; and it furnishes the explanation of the well-known fact that he who does the wrong is always harder to be won to reconciliation than he who received the injury. Indeed, to such an extent is this the case, that only when the hearts of both are softened by a sense of their obligation to God for His forgiveness, can there be anything like a permanent or unsuspicious healing of the breach between them. To be able to forgive, one must first himself have received forgiveness from God; and he who has tasted the Divine favour, and knows how the reception of *that* disposes the heart to the love of others, will be the frankest also in his acceptance of forgiveness at the hands of him whom he has injured. The closer a man's walk with God is, the more will he be disposed to deal forgivingly with those who wrong him; but human magnanimity will always be suspected by those who have not yet appreciated the Divine. The men who believe most thoroughly in human depravity, and, along with that, in Divine mercy, are those who are most tender in their dealings with wrong-doers; while those who have greatest faith in what they call the dignity of human nature, and have not learned the meaning of the cross, are always the most suspicious of their fellows. It seems to be a strange paradox, and yet it is the simple truth.

The brothers here could not understand, as they certainly did not appreciate, the character of Joseph. But though they erred in that, they took the proper course in making immediate application to himself on the subject. They did not go to him directly, but approached him at first, at least, through the medium of another—most probably, perhaps, Benjamin—who said, in their behalf, " Thy father did command before he died, saying, so shall ye say unto Joseph, Forgive, I pray thee now, the trespass

of thy brethren, and their sin ; for they did unto thee evil :
and now, we pray thee, forgive the trespass of the servants
of the God of thy father." Some have insinuated that in
causing their advocate to speak thus they were guilty of
falsehood, since there is no mention in the narrative of
Jacob's saying anything of this sort to them. But that
only shows to what ridiculous lengths the argument from
silence, never very satisfactory at the best, may be driven ;
for we have in this history, interesting as it is, the merest
outline of the lives of those to whom it refers, and in two
of the verses of this chapter we have the events of sixty
years summarised. How absurd, therefore, it is to argue
that because in such an epitome as this record is we have
no account of Jacob's ever saying this to his sons, therefore he never said it ! Besides, on an occasion like this
the brothers were not likely to go to Joseph with a falsehood in their mouths. It is quite probable, therefore, that
in the anticipation of their father's death they had spoken
to him of their fear lest, after his departure, Joseph might
punish them for their sin, and that he had advised or
commanded them to take the course which they were now
following. Moreover, they knew that the fact that their
father had so counselled them would have immense weight
with Joseph, and therefore they made distinct mention of
it in their plea. Nor did they use that name in vain, for
" Joseph wept when they spake unto him." Their words
opened up again a painful chapter in his history, and
brought to bear upon that the memory of the grief which
had convulsed his heart at the death of his father, while
at the same time they revealed that he was even yet an
object of suspicion and distrust to his brothers. " Have
I been so long time with you, and yet hast thou not known
me, Philip ? " said the Lord to His disciple, in answer to a
question which indicated the spiritual obtuseness of the
apostle ; and similarly here Joseph might have said, " Have

you been so long time with me, the sharers of my prosperity, and the objects of my constant care, and yet do you not know me better than to have such unworthy thoughts concerning me? When have I given you any ground for cherishing such unworthy sentiments regarding me?" But there were no words of objurgation. The only reproof he addressed to them was in his tears; and as they—once again unconsciously fulfilling the old dream —fell down before his face, he re-assured them with these words, "Fear not: for am I in the place of God? But as for you, ye thought evil against me; but God meant it unto good, to bring to pass, as it is this day, to save much people alive. Now therefore fear ye not: I will nourish you, and your little ones." Joseph regarded it as the special prerogative of God to punish iniquity, and he would not attempt to take the Divine law into his own hands. It was not his either to punish or to forgive wrong so far as it was sin. Instead, therefore, of coming to him they ought to go to God. Then, so far as the injury to himself was concerned, it was, to be sure, hard enough to bear at the time, but then God had brought so much good out of it, both to himself and to others, that he had come now to look upon it as only a needed step towards the great honour of his life, and therefore he cherished no enmity towards them because of it, and they need have no fear whatever of his dealing harshly with them. He would continue to do as he had done ever since their removal to Egypt, and would nourish them and their little ones with all tenderness and affection.

" Ye thought evil against me; but God meant it unto good"—that is the golden lesson that comes out of this whole history. The Providence of God was in and over every incident in it, making them all co-operate for the bringing about of the great design which He had for the deliverance of the people in famine, for the education of the children of Israel in Egypt, and for the unification of them at length into a nation capable of taking possession of the Land of Promise. We have had occasion frequently to mark how the superintendence of God regulates the events of nature, even without any miraculous intervention with what are called natural laws, and repeatedly in this history we have noticed how the common and ordinary operations of these laws have been so adjusted and combined as to bring out results that were clearly designed, the supernatural thus working in and through the natural. But the special point in Joseph's words here is, that the same control is exercised by God in and over the actions of men. They are free agents, conscious of no constraint, and seeking only their own things, yet through the prosecution by them of their own selfish and sinful ends God works out at length His own holy and benevolent purposes. These brothers were eager only to get rid of Joseph, and at first thought to kill him; but one of their number persuaded them to put him into a pit, and another, having the thing apparently suggested to him at the moment, by what seemed the accidental presence of the trading Ishmaelites, proposed to sell him to them. This was agreed to by the rest and consented to by the Ishmaelites, and so he was taken to Egypt. Now see how many wills—all of them free—were concerned in this matter, and how at length, through the evil intentions and actions of his brothers, and the selfish gain-seeking of the Ishmaelites, God carried forward His purpose for Joseph's elevation, and the emigration of Jacob and his sons to Egypt. The same thing comes out in connection with his imprisonment in Egypt. Potiphar's wife was seeking only to gratify her revenge when she concocted the lie with which she imposed upon her husband, and Potiphar himself was taking means for the wreaking out of his anger when he sent him to the dungeon. Yet here again, through all these self-seeking actions of theirs, God was bringing Joseph only so much the nearer to Pharaoh and his ultimate position by the monarch's side. Once more the chief butler and chief baker were working for their own ends when they did what offended their master, and he was only thinking of their punishment when he put them into the prison ; yet in the conjunction of their presence there with that of Joseph we see one of the critical hinges on which the history turns, and can perceive the purpose of God working itself out through the agency of men. If you ask me *how* this is done without infringing on human freedom, I frankly answer that I cannot tell ; but that it *was* done in this history is abundantly plain. And this history is not by any means exceptional in that regard. Assyria, as we read in Isaiah,* was employed by Jehovah as His instrument for the punishment of Israel ; yet it said concerning Him, " Howbeit He meaneth not so, neither doth His heart think so ; but it is in His heart to destroy and cut off nations not a few." But, perhaps, in no one event in human history is this truth so clearly illustrated as in the crucifixion of our Lord and Saviour Jesus Christ. Thus Peter speaks in his Pentecostal sermon : " Him, being delivered by the determinate counsel and foreknowledge of God, ye have taken, and by wicked hands have crucified and slain." † Now, if these words have any meaning at all, they assert that all the events connected with the crucifixion of the Lord were foreplanned and foretold, and that God was in them, controlling them so as to make them work together for a certain result, while yet the agents in them were acting freely from their own motives, and therefore wickedly. Now, although I cannot explain how this is secured, and will not be enticed into any attempt to do so, I have been

---

* Isaiah x. 5-7.   † Acts ii. 23.

the more particular to bring out the fact that the actions of men are under the control of God, because it is in this department that our faith in Providence is weakest. When a fellow-man injures us we are apt to say, that if it had been a dispensation of Providence we could have borne it, but that this is beyond endurance.   Now of course there is an immense difference between what God does directly and what He simply permits others to do; yet the fact that the actions so permitted are wrought into His plan of our lives and made to help it forward to its fulfilment, ought surely to have some importance in our view, and ought to lead us at once to humble resignation to God's will, and hearty forgiveness of those who may have injured us.   This was the view of David when Shimei cursed him; for he said, "Let him curse, for the Lord hath bidden him."*   This also was the view of the Christians at Cesarea; for, after they had heard the prophecy of Agabus, and had in vain importuned Paul not to go to Jerusalem, it is written, "And when he would not be persuaded, we ceased, saying, The will of the Lord be done."†   That is to say, they recognised the Providence and will of God in the Apostle's unyielding determination, and submitted to it as such.   The same principle is acknowledged in the common proverb, to the effect that "man proposes, but God disposes"; and it seems to me that if we were more constantly to remember it, we should find it easier to possess our souls in patience and in peace, even under the ill-treatment to which men may subject us.   It does not diminish the guilt of those who wrong us, but it does give us a staff to support us under the wrong; for it reminds us that God is over all, and it leads us to look for some result of good from our present humiliation.

---

* 2 Samuel xv. 11.   † Acts xxi. 14.

Now if these things are true, it follows that nothing in our lives is really untoward, but that everything gives its own quotum towards the good result that God has planned for us. Here is the "open secret" of that marvellous equanimity which is so characteristic of Joseph from first to last. We understand now why he was neither overwhelmed by the calamities of his youthful years, nor made giddy by the greatness to which in his latter days he was exalted. Wherever he was, and whatever happened to him, he had the unfaltering conviction that "God meant it unto good"; and if we had the same trust in the wise and loving arrangements of an all-superintending God, we, too, might continue peaceful amid all the changes and surprises of our early lives. Whoso has this faith may sing with tranquil heart these simple lines:

> Father, I know that all my life
> Is portioned out by Thee;
> And the changes that are sure to come
> I do not fear to see;
> But I ask Thee for a present mind
> Intent on pleasing Thee.

And now we leap over an interval of sixty-one years, during which all we know of Joseph and his brethren is comprised in these two verses: "And Joseph dwelt in Egypt, he, and his father's house: and Joseph lived an hundred and ten years. And Joseph saw Ephraim's children of the third generation"—that is, as it seems to me, Ephraim's great-grandchildren—"the children also of Machir the son of Manasseh"—that is, Manasseh's grandchildren—"were brought up upon Joseph's knees." He lived ninety-three years in Egypt, and eighty of these were subsequent to his elevation to the second place in the kingdom. There were, probably, a succession of Pharaohs on the throne, after the passing away of the monarch whom he had first served so signally during the time of famine; and it is

likely that to the last he retained the confidence and
affection both of the royal family and of the people at
large. But in the absence of any particulars we may not
attempt to make history by conjecture.

But the time drew nigh when he, too, must die and this
is the last record concerning him : "Joseph said unto his
brethren, I die : and God will surely visit you, and bring
you out of this land unto the land which He sware to
Abraham, to Isaac, and to Jacob. And Joseph took an
oath of the children of Israel, saying, God will surely visit
you, and ye shall carry up my bones from hence. So
Joseph died, being an hundred and ten years old : and they
embalmed him, and he was put in a coffin in Egypt."
Not buried, as I judge, but embalmed and put into a
mummy-case, which was kept in some one of the homes of
his kindred.

Now here we are struck at once with the resemblance
of Joseph's words to those of Jacob in one part, and their
difference from them in another. Jacob said, " Behold, I
die; but God shall be with you, and bring you again unto
the land of your fathers," just as Joseph said, " I die : and
God will surely visit you, and bring you out of this land
unto the land which He sware to Abraham, to Isaac, and
to Jacob." But while Jacob requested that his body
should be at once buried in Machpelah, Joseph required
that his bones should remain among the Israelites, and be
taken with them when they should go to Canaan. Both
alike were animated by faith in the covenant and oath of
God, that their descendants should possess the Promised
Land, but Jacob showed his faith by asking to be immediately buried in the sepulchre of his fathers, while
Joseph manifested his by leaving his bones among his
people, and giving commandment that they should be
carried up with them out of Egypt. And if you will look
at the difference of situation between the two, you will find

the explanation of the difference between the two requests. For Jacob and his sons had been already long in Canaan. It was natural for them, therefore, to dwell on the memories of the past; and Jacob, by asking to be buried immediately in Machpelah, virtually said to his sons, " Do not forget Canaan in Egypt. Let not the prosperity of the present drown out of your heart all love for the past, or all longing for a return to its happiness. Keep alive the memory of the good land that is for the moment behind you"; and for that purpose, knowing how affection clusters round the sepulchre of a father, he had his body taken at once to Hebron. But when Joseph came to die, the majority of the descendants of Jacob had never seen Canaan. They had grown up in Egypt, and their danger was that of settling down there in contentment, without having any desire to go to the land of their fathers. Therefore, to keep alive among them the truth that they were yet to go to Canaan, and to preserve in the midst of them the evidence of his faith that they should ultimately possess that land, he left his body, embalmed, yet unburied, among them, with the instruction that when they did go they should take it along with them. They say that at the feasts of Egypt it was usual to bring a mummy to the table, that the guests might be reminded thereby of their mortality. But Joseph here left his coffined body to his people, that by its presence among them, and preservation by them, they might never forget that Egypt was not their final resting-place—their national home—and might be stimulated to hold themselves in constant readiness to arise and go to their own land. Thus, though the expression of the faith in the two cases was different, it was in each appropriate to the circumstances of those to whom it was made.

And now, how was this request of Joseph's fulfilled? Read with me these two passages, and you will see: " And

Moses took the bones of Joseph with him: for he had straitly sworn the children of Israel, saying, God will surely visit you; and ye shall carry up my bones away hence with you."* It was a terrible night. The destroying angel had passed through Egypt and laid low the first-born in every household. The panic-stricken Pharaoh had ordered the Israelites away at once, and they started in great haste. Yet even in that crisis they did not forget the descending obligation of the oath which their fathers had sworn to Joseph, and they took time to carry with them his remains. Read again: "And the bones of Joseph, which the children of Israel brought up out of Egypt, buried they in Shechem, in a parcel of ground which Jacob bought of the sons of Hamor the father of Shechem for an hundred pieces of silver: and it became the inheritance of the children of Joseph."† Thus, between the death and burial of Joseph an interval of probably from three to four hundred years elapsed, during all of which his remains were kept by the children of Israel, a witness to the faith by which he was animated, and a prophecy of their ultimate possession of the land of Canaan, so that the author of the Epistle to the Hebrews had a right to say, "By faith Joseph, when he died, made mention of the departing of the children of Israel; and gave commandment concerning his bones."‡

And now, leaving the character and career of Joseph to form the subject of a separate chapter, let us conclude by giving prominence to the lesson conveyed to us in these parting words, "*I die: and God will surely visit you.*" They bring before us the contrast between the mortality of men and the eternity of God. They die, but He abides "the King eternal, immortal, the only wise God." Very strikingly is this fact illustrated in the sacred Scriptures,

---

* Exodus xiii. 19.   † Joshua xxiv. 32.   ‡ Hebrews xi. 22.

in which there is only one name that keeps its place in the forefront from the beginning to the end. For a time we read of Adam; then of Noah; then of Abraham, of Isaac, and of Jacob; then of Joseph; then of Moses; then of Joshua. After that we have the age of the Judges; then that of the Kings and Prophets; then that of the Captivity; then that of the Restoration, under Ezra, Nehemiah, Haggai, Zechariah, and Malachi. Then in the New Testament we have Apostles and Evangelists. But throughout we have over all the Living and Eternal God. One generation goeth and another cometh, but He abideth for ever. This great man or that may give his name to an epoch, but God's Providence is over all alike. He is in the Bible, as He is in the universe, omnipresent, giving its unity to the Book, as He does to human history as a whole, and rounding it all out into that great circle whose ample circumference sweeps from "Paradise Lost" to "Paradise Regained." If, therefore, as we read these pages, we are continually oppressed with the mortality of man, and reminded of the dirge of Moses—" Thou carriest them away as with a flood: they are as a sleep; in the morning they are as grass that groweth up; in the morning it flourisheth and groweth up; in the evening it is cut down and withereth." "We spend our years as a tale that is told " —we are comforted also with the great consolation, "Lord, Thou hast been our dwelling-place in all generations. Before the mountains were brought forth, or even Thou hadst formed the earth and the world, even from everlasting to everlasting Thou art God."

Nay more, by the course of the Bible history He lets us see that an individual life, however fragmentary or incomplete it may seem to be to human view, fits into His comprehensive plan and is not lived in vain. As we pass from one to another, and stand now by the dying Abraham, again by the departing Jacob, and still again by Joseph at

he is passing away, we are not permitted to think of any
one man as indispensable; but neither, on the other hand,
are we allowed to suppose that their work has been in
vain, for God is in and over all, and the life of every good
man becomes a part of that great whole which is to be,
at last, the revelation and vindication, as well as the
consummation, of the mystery of Providence. We may
have some little difficulty in seeing this in regard to ourselves, because the microscopic minuteness of our individual
parts does not give us a good opportunity of observing
their relation to other and larger interests; but we have
no such perplexity in reference to those whose biographies
are set before us in the Scriptures; and standing as we do
now beside the coffin of him whose history we have
been studying, it is fitting that we should recognise the
comforting fact that each one leaves his own little bit of
work on the great edifice which God is rearing through
the centuries, and which is to be at last for His own
habitation through the Spirit. We lose sight of that amid
the trivialities, as we account them, of our personal
histories, and so God has put the lives of other men here,
as it were, under the magnifying-glass of an inspired record,
that from the very largeness of the scale we may be at no
loss to discover the point and value of the lesson.

Now this truth is full of comfort, on the one hand to
the dying servant of God, and, on the other, to the
bereaved who are called to mourn his loss. It is full
of comfort to the dying, for whatever of good he has done
in the world shall not be lost when he is gone. In the
words of the appropriate inscription on the monument
to the Wesleys in Westminster Abbey, " God buries the
workers, but He carries on the work." When Moses dies,
God has Joshua fully trained to take his place. When
Elijah steps into the chariot that is to take him to glory,
God has Elisha there in readiness to receive his falling

mantle. When Stephen is stoned to death, Paul is prepared by God to take up his mission. Thus, though
the man disappears, his work is carried forward and is,
through the energising influence of God's spirit, made
operative all through the ages. The sower may die, but
the seed which fell from his hands matures into a harvest
which is reaped by others, and becomes in its turn the
food of multitudes and the germ of many harvests more.
I stood once on a Highland hill and marked a spot upon
the landscape greener than all else around. When I
inquired into the reason, I learned that for many, many
years there had been a village there, and that the gardens
of the villagers, so long under cultivation, kept unwonted
verdure still. So, through the operations of God's grace,
the earth is greener where His servants have been at work,
though the servants themselves have long since passed
away. The operations of grace, like those of Nature, go
on after men have died, because God lives to maintain
them and nothing done for Him is ever allowed to come to
nothing. So when we are called to leave the earth, the
work in which we delighted shall not be lost. We die,
but God lives; and we may be sure that under His care it
will flourish. Ay, perhaps the handful of corn which we
have cast on the top of the mountains, amid many
discouragements, and apparently on a barren soil, may
spring up, so that "the fruit thereof shall shake like
Lebanon." And the same thing holds true of the loved
ones whom we are called to leave on earth. God remains
to take care of them, so that we may say to them as
Joseph did to his kinsmen, "I die: but God will surely
visit you." Though he have no other legacy to leave
them, the dying Christian can leave his God to his
children, and is not that enough? Earthly guardians
may prove unfaithful to their trust, and may, through
covetousness, rob the widow and the orphans who have

been committed to their care; but "the Lord is mindful of His own," and they who are His wards are always under His protection. They may have many hardships, and it may seem for a while as if He had forgotten them, just as the Israelites had hard bondage in the land of Egypt; but when "the tale of bricks is doubled then comes Moses," and he will not suffer them always to be oppressed. Therefore, when we are in departing, let us take comfort in the thought that the covenant of Jehovah is with us and with our children, and that He remains to keep that covenant with those whom we leave behind us.

Then what consolation comes from the eternity of God to those who are bereaved? I have quoted already from the ninetieth Psalm, but its significance in this relation is too marked to be left out of sight. It was written by Moses in the wilderness, when he was depressed by the death of those who had reached man's estate when he led them out of Egypt. There came a time when he was left wellnigh alone of all his generation; and then he took his comfort out of the permanence of God, singing, " Lord, Thou hast been our dwelling-place in all generations; from everlasting to everlasting Thou art God," and by that he was upheld. We see the same thing in David's case; for not far from the close of his life, and when many of his early companions had gone into "the silent land," he wrote the eighteenth Psalm, in which he said, " The Lord liveth, and blessed be my Rock; and let the God of my salvation be exalted." Yes, "the Lord liveth," therefore let us not refuse to be comforted when dear ones are taken from our side. He *can* sustain us and He *will*. He is as near us as He was when they were with us, and they were but the agents whom He used for our welfare. But He is not tied to any instrumentality, and He can guide, uphold, and bless by one as well as by another. He takes away the earthly prop that we may learn to lean the more thoroughly on

Himself. "He will surely visit us"; yea, He will be ever with us, and when our death-hour comes we shall be with Him. "Happy are the people who are in such a case; yea, happy is the people whose God is the Lord." With these feelings in our hearts, we can surely give our hearty Amen to Paul's doxology, "Now unto the King eternal, immortal, invisible, the only wise God, be honour and glory for ever and ever. Amen."

XV.

THE CHARACTER AND CAREER OF JOSEPH.

GENESIS xlv. 8.

THE history of Joseph, on the consideration of which we have been so long engaged, differs from all the others which are given at any length in the book of Genesis, in that we are permitted to follow it almost uninterruptedly from boyhood to old age. This is one secret of its charm, especially for young readers; the rather, because the qualities which appear in him at first are seen only to grow with his growth and to strengthen with his strength. In him the adage was pre-eminently true that "the boy is father of the man"; and though his life had its trials and discouragements, the conflicts which he had to wage were all external. There was little in him of that antagonism between the spirit and the flesh of which the Christian apostle speaks. From the very first he seems to have been whole-heartedly on the side of God, and his struggles were not with himself in order to maintain that undivided allegiance, so much as they were with others because he was determined to preserve it. His character, indeed, was not perfect, but there was less of alloy in it than in that of most men. We see in it less of the alternation between good and evil, between strength and weakness, than there is in the majority of those whose biographies are given us in this honest book. There is no wavering irresolution, no petulant impatience, no unscrupulous self-seeking; and if he never rose to those heights of spiritual communion with his God to which Abraham and Jacob were exalted, he never sank to the depths of deceit into which both of these patriarchs sometimes descended.   His career is uniquely interesting as that of a good boy who was not a weakling; that of a pious man who was not a business failure; and that of a great man who, in the glory of his exaltation, did not outgrow the simplicity of his youth.

In many of its features it bears a striking resemblance to that of Daniel at a later day.   As Auberlen has said, " The one stands at the commencement, the other at the end of the Jewish history of revelation; they were both representatives of the true God and His people at heathen courts ; both were exemplary in their pure walk before the Lord ; both were endowed with the gift of bringing into clear light the dim presentiments of truth which express themselves among the heathen in God-sent dreams ; both were gifted with marvellous wisdom and insight, and for this reason highly honoured among the nations."* But with this general resemblance there were specific differences; and it may be profitable, in drawing this series of discourses to a close, to spend a little time in the attempt to analyse the character of Joseph, and unfold, so far as we may, the secret both of its goodness and its greatness.

Beginning at the beginning, we are at once impressed with his devotion to his father.   The boy, early motherless, was taken, not for that reason alone, but also for the sake of Rachel herself, to his father's heart, and the intercourse between them seems to have been of the closest and most confidential kind ; indeed, there is something of idylic beauty in the companionship of the two.   We

---

* " Daniel and the Revelation," by C. A. Auberlen.   Translated by Rev. A. Saphir, D.D., pp. 23, 24.

find the boy at home with his father when all his half-
brothers were absent, and the coat of distinction which
his father unwisely gave him was an indication of the love
he bore him; while the commission to proceed to
Shechem may be taken as an illustration of the kind of
confidence which his father placed in him. Then, in the
frank rehearsal of his dreams we have an exemplification,
on the other hand, of the open and unchecked freedom
with which Joseph was accustomed to deal with his father.
Now, if we may regard these as typical instances, they
suggest a great deal more that is not recorded. They permit us to believe that in their familiar fellowship Jacob
would tell Joseph the chief events in his own personal
history, and specially those chapters in it of which Bethel
and Peniel were the scenes. We are sure, too, that when
the conversation on these subjects was exhausted the
father and son would adjourn together to the tent of Isaac
to hear again from the lips of the blind old grandfather
the story of that terrible experience on Moriah, when,
through the arrested sacrifice of his own son, Abraham
saw down through the ages into the mystery of Calvary.
Revelation, then, was a personal privilege which he who
received could share with others only through oral communication; and so these stories heard by Joseph from
the lips of Isaac and of Jacob were to him what the Bible
now is to our children. Through them he learned to know
of God, and so the thought of God became in his mind
inseparably associated with his father. His father was all
the dearer to him because of the revelation of God which
he received through him, and he was all the dearer to his
father because of the readiness with which he accepted the
truth thus communicated, and obeyed the Lord thus
made known to him. Thus natural affection was
sweetened, elevated, and purified by spiritual communion,
and it may be that the two were drawn together all the

more closely by the fact that the other members of the family at that time seemed to care for none of these things. In any case, they were more to each other than either of them was to any of the rest. And when, after a long interval of separation, they were brought together again, the old footing between them was at once restored. We cannot quite understand, indeed, the unbroken silence maintained by Joseph towards his father for so many years ; but, whatever caused that, we are sure that it was no estrangement of heart from him, for when they saw each other again they rushed at once into each other's arms, and all the old tenderness came out between them.

No matter how old a man he may be, the true son is always a boy again when he is beside his father ; and no matter how venerable a man the son may be to others, his aged father still regards him as his boy. That is true to-day, and, thank God, it is a familiar truth to many of us ; but just because of that we are all the more delighted to find an exemplification of it here, in those visits paid by Joseph, when he was an Egyptian grandee, to his venerable sire. It is a beautiful trait, this filial devotion, as honourable to the father as it is to the son, and regarded, too, by God with benignant complacency, for the precept " Honour thy father and thy mother " is " the first commandment with promise." Let this then be the first of our lessons from the career of Joseph. Fathers, take your sons into friendly, confidential, religious fellowship with yourselves. Sons, cultivate companionship with your fathers, that you may learn what God has been to them, and He may become doubly precious to you as " your father's God." The covenant holds yet, and it counts for something to be a covenant child.

But now, as the result of this fellowship with his father, and this reception of God's revelation through him, we mark next in Joseph a constant recognition of the presence of God with him. That, indeed, seems to me to be the one great, all-dominating consciousness of his life. He believed in God, not as afar off, but as always near; not as sitting aloof from all the actions of men, but as overruling and controlling them ; not as an enemy to be feared, but as a friend to be loved and trusted and served. No persecution could keep him from realising that God was with him, and no prosperity could blind him to the fact that it was to God he owed it all. It seems to me, as I read his history, that it was a constant " walk with God." His faith had almost the strength of sight. That which his father wrestled for as a great privilege, and enjoyed for but a brief season, in a special theophany, he seemed constantly to realise by faith, so that he could say, " I see God face to face and my life is preserved." Or if such a description appears extravagant, we may at least declare that what was true of Moses was true also of him, and that he not only " endured," but lived " as seeing him who is invisible." He felt that the Lord was round about him, and whatever men might intend he knew that God always " meant it unto good." Now this faith in the constant presence of God with him enabled him to maintain that evenliness of disposition on which again and again we have remarked. It kept him from being either very much depressed by adversity or exceedingly elated by prosperity. He did not indeed stoically take things good and bad as they came, neither did he accept them thoughtlessly as matters of course, but he received them as from the hand of God, and was confident that He would yet reveal to him the purpose for which He sent them. Hence, though his heart was wrung with anguish when he was cast into the pit, he did not indulge in unavailing regrets ; and though " the iron entered into his soul" when he was in the dungeon, he was able patiently to wait for God's time for his deliverance.

But neither did he forget the Lord's hand in his prosperity.
That was as undeserved by him as his adversity had been.
Both alike came from the Most High, and in both alike God
"meant it unto good." So, while he was kept from despondency in the one experience, he was preserved from pride
in the other. He was not self-poised but God-poised. The
balance of his nature was God. That kept him always in
equilibrio, so that he was still the same man in simplicity,
humility, and calmness, whether he was ministering to the
prisoners in the round house or riding in the second chariot
of the king. God was with him in the dungeon, and that
kept him from over-estimating its hardships ; God was with
him in the chariot, and that kept him from over-estimating
its honour. The affliction did not sour his heart, and the
prosperity did not turn his head, because in both he felt
that God was near him ; and when we get to such a faith as
he had in the presence and protection of a covenant God,
we shall be able to preserve an equanimity like his.

Nor must I forget to add here that this sense of the
nearness of God to him lay at the root of that moral
courage with which he was endowed. He did not fear to
tell of his brother's misdeeds, no matter how they might
threaten him, for God was on his side ; and when temptation assailed him he had no difficulty in resisting it, because
he felt that God was near. "How shall I do this great
wickedness and sin against God ?" these were his words :
and the sin was felt to be so heinous, not because God was
present to take note of it, but because the God who was
present had been his constant Friend, and was his omni-
potent Protector.

So again he could enter in before Pharaoh without trepidation, because he was always consciously in the
presence of the King of kings ; and he had no misgivings
about undertaking the management of public affairs during
the years of plenty and of famine, because he knew that

the Lord would " stand by him and strengthen him."
Brethren, there is nothing that so largely contributes to
what is commonly called " presence of mind " in danger
or in difficulty as this sense of the constant nearness of
God to us. He who possesses that faith has always God
in reserve, and therefore he is always as calm as Elisha
was in Dothan, and as courageous as Daniel was before
Darius.

Still further, Joseph's constant recognition of the
presence of God with him gave him patience to wait God's
time, and piety to take God's way for his promotion in life.
Very early in life there came to him the Divine premonition
that there was a great future before him. It was not simply
the consciousness that he had it " in him " to do something noble, and attain to something exalted in the world.
I acknowledge, indeed, that such feelings in many have
been the prophecies of exaltation, and have so fired ambition that they have, so to say, become the means of their
own fulfilment at a later date. But Joseph's early visions
came to him directly from God. They were the same in
kind as the Divine communications that were made to
Abraham and Isaac and Jacob, and they were given to
him in a manner that was special, and distinct from all
ordinary forecasts of the future. But he did not try to
help on their attainment by improper means, neither was
he in eager haste to have them fulfilled. He let God take
His time, and he did not seek, like Rebekah, to help him
out in a sinful way. He " waited" on the Lord, and while
he waited he worked just at what his hand found to do, and
in a manner that was strictly irreproachable and upright.
He would take no " short cuts " to success. He knew
nothing of vaulting into greatness by some sudden and
spasmodic leap, to be just as suddenly overturned because
he was not fitted for the work to which he had aspired.
But he kept plodding on, always doing his best, whether

as a shepherd, or as a household steward, or as a prison warden; and so when he was called to be the Grand Vizier, he did his best there too, and it was such a "*best*" as piloted the country safely through a crisis which else might have resulted in general starvation or in the wildest anarchy and confusion.

But why was he always doing his best? Because, as you may clearly see, if you care to read between the lines of the record, he was always working for God. That kept him from indolence; that prevented him from indulging in murmuring impatience; that preserved him from staining his record with anything like dishonesty or iniquity. To him, indeed, as to a greater than he, or than all of us, long afterwards, the Devil came and offered the kingdom and the glory if He would but fall down and worship him; for the strength of the temptation presented by Potiphar's wife, to such an one as he, lay not in its appeal to fleshly appetite so much as in the fact that it opened up a way by which he might speedily reach the summit of his ambition, while yet the thing required of him was not regarded in Egypt as any great enormity. But he spurned it from him, saying, in another form, yet virtually what the Saviour said, "Get thee behind me, Satan, for I shall worship the Lord my God, and Him only shall I serve"; and he went back, to go a long way round, a way which led through a prison, and which took him years to traverse, but a way that led at length to unsullied greatness, which, once attained, was kept by him for life. Oh, young men, what an example there is here for you! It tells you to keep ever alive within you the consciousness that God is at your side. It bids you remember that it is with God you have to do. It urges you to "make haste slowly"; that is, to make haste in God's way, and never to be guilty of doing evil that good may come. "Strait is the gate and narrow is the way"

to the greatness that God confers. His path to honour
and influence and power is still steep and arduous and
rugged, and evermore, as you toil on and up, some
emissary of the Devil will come and suggest to you a
shorter and easier way; but believe him not, for he will
lead you through a swamp, in which it will go hard if you
do not sink and disappear: or, if he give you what he
promises, he will give it but for a little season, after which
will come a sudden and irremediable collapse. You do
not need to do more than read the newspapers of last
week to see how true that is. Oh, that you would lay it
to heart, and be content in your business as in your closet
to " wait upon the Lord." " He that believeth " will
make no such " haste " as that—he will bide God's time;
and if he can rise only by using the Devil's means, he will
be content to remain for ever as he is and where he is;
for, after all, character is the real success, and the man
who can say " No " to the Devil is a hero, even if the
saying of it should send him, in the first instance, to a
gaol. But commonly God does not leave such heroes in
the dungeon, for after the prison comes the royal chariot,
and it comes to stay, or if it do not come on earth, there
is in heaven a crown that fadeth not away. Serve God,
then, where you are with constant diligence and unswerving
loyalty, and leave all else to Him.

But, as another result of this constant sense of God's
presence which Joseph cherished, I name his forgiving
spirit. He had come to see that through all the evil that
men intended to do him, God was working towards his
great good end, of setting him near the throne of Egypt,
and saving much people alive, and so that made him
ready to pardon his brothers for their cruel treatment of
him in his early life. True, he took means to satisfy himself of their repentance, but when he was convinced of
that he at once made himself known to them, and took

them again to his heart.   Now I verily believe that if we
had anything like Joseph's faith in the universality of
God's providence we should find it more easy to forgive
those who have done us wrong; and as that is one of the
hardest things to do, it might be well for us to cultivate
the faith which makes it easy.   We are too ready to
forgive with reservation.   If, like David, we consent to
Absalom's recall, we add the condition that he shall not
look upon our face; and there is too much in us of the spirit
of the Highlandman who, having been brought, on what
was supposed to be his death-bed, to forgive a neighbour
with whom he had a feud, and who had been led into his
chamber for a formal reconciliation, called after him as
he was leaving the room, " Mind, if I get better this will
be all off ! "   But Joseph forgave right out, and he did so
because he knew that God had made the cruelty of his
brothers to work out his good, and because he felt that
God was a witness to his forgiving act.   Now, when to
these considerations we add this other—more clearly
revealed to us than it was to Joseph—that God has forgiven us freely and fully all our sins, we ought to find it
more blessed to give forgiveness than it is to receive it,
and should have our delight in dealing with others as our
God has dealt with us.

Thus regarded, we see that the character of Joseph was
in every particular the evolution of his realisation of the
nearness of God and his faith in the universality of His
providence, and that for these he was indebted to the
revelation that came to him in early life through Jacob
and Isaac.

And in concluding I would draw attention to two
points.   The first is that Joseph's early piety was not
incompatible with strength and manliness of character.
I am particular to set that clearly before you, for it has
come to be believed by the young people of these days

that piety is a simpering, sentimental thing, betokening the existence both of physical and mental weakness in him by whom it is manifested. Something of this impression perhaps may be due to the influence of those books for juveniles which tell of "good boys" who had little or nothing of boyhood about them, and dropped into early graves. Thus the idea is fostered that when one becomes an earnest Christian in the years of his boyhood, he is "too good for this world," and is removed as soon as may be to a better. Now such books are unhealthy, because they are untrue; and the mischief is that they tend to repel their readers from religion altogether. Young people do not want to become Christians if their histories are to be of that sort. They are conscious of the possession of overflowing vitality, and they have, besides, the natural and laudable ambition to do something to purpose in the world.

They shrink, therefore, from a life of physical weakness and from an early death, and they should be told of the early piety of those who have lived to a good old age, and who were honoured to do good and noble service for God and their generation. Now that is what they find in the biography of Joseph, for he gave himself to God as a boy, but lived to be an hundred and ten years old, and for more than three-fourths of his days he occupied the second place in the land of Egypt. There was no element of feebleness about him. He was healthy alike in body and in mind. He had the courage not only to have convictions, but also to act upon them. He was a manly boy, and, as we have seen, there was to the last also much of the boy even in his manhood. Now I am anxious that the young people of my audience should take heed to these things. You will make a tremendous mistake if you suppose that piety unfits you for life, or imagine that its existence in youth

is an abnormal thing which indicates the presence of
disease.   Believe me, there is nothing so wholesome for
you as to give yourselves early to the Lord.   It will lay
in you the foundation of a vigorous and energetic character.   It will bring the highest and holiest of all motives to
bear alike on education, recreation, and business, and
enable you to make the very best of yourselves for God
and for your fellow-men.   From every point of view,
therefore, such a history as this of Joseph should en-
courage you to early piety.   It bids you consecrate yourselves to the Saviour ere yet " the cares of the world " or
" the deceitfulness of riches " have stolen away your
hearts.   It proves to you that piety is by no means incompatible with manliness.   It gives you the promise of many
days of usefulness and honour in the world, and illustrates
how truly Paul did write when he said, " Godliness is
profitable unto all things, having the promise both of the
life that now is, and also of that which is to come."

Finally, I desire to place fully in your view this other
fact, namely, that Joseph, even in the world's sense of the
word, was a successful man.   He had his struggles and
his trials, but still, at the early age of thirty, he reached a
position of honour and emolument which was second only
to that of the Egyptian monarch, and he retained that, so
far as appears, to the end.   Now, of course, his was in
some respects an exceptional case.   But it was not exceptional in this, that though a good man, he became a
successful man, for in the word of God we have similar
instances in the lives of Daniel and Nehemiah ; and in our
own day and in our own land we can point to not a few
who are equally remarkable for their Christian character
and their business eminence.   It is, I know, a common
idea among many that religion and success, commercial
or professional, are incompatible.   If one have the
reputation of being a godly man, he is by multitudes

written down as unfitted for attaining the highest kind of
commercial success; and, on the other hand, if one have
risen to eminence as a merchant or a statesman, it is
supposed that he cannot be a very devout man. But I
cannot admit that either of these imputations is true.
Why should the cultivation of the heart be inconsistent
with eminence in commerce or in public life, any more
than the gratification of a taste for literature? Yet how
many men are equally eminent in both departments. The
noblest statesman that Great Britain has seen for more
than a generation has been able, without detracting from
his influence either as a financial reformer or as a prime-
minister, to cultivate Homeric studies and enrich literature
by many valuable essays. Nay, I will add that he is as
eminent as a Christian as he is in either of the other two
respects, so that in his case also the cultivation of the
heart has been as little incompatible with his greatness as
his devotion to literature.

But, more than this, the very duties of business furnish
an opportunity for the fostering of religion. For what is
religion? Is it not, above all other things, the science of
character? Is it not the process of self-formation according
to the purest model, from the loftiest motives, and with
the best assistance? And if that be so, does not public
life give the noblest opportunities for its prosecution?
Whatever we do, and wherever we are, we are either
making or manifesting character, and we must do so either
in the right way or in the wrong. Religion is the doing of
this in the right way, and if that be incompatible with
success in business, then all I have to say is, so much
the worse for business. But it is not incompatible with
business success. It may not give a rapid fortune, indeed,
but that is not a misfortune, for these rapid fortunes often
end in prison or in exile. But it has often given, and it
will give again, solid, substantial, enduring prosperity,

which no panic can sweep away. Nor is this all. Consider what religion does for a man. It brings him under the influence of the most powerful motives; it opens his eyes to the sight of the invisible; it leads him to work, as Joseph did all through, with the consciousness that God is at his side. But is there anything in that to paralyze industry or to overlay diligence? Nay, verily, for he who is doing business for God will always be in earnest. His dilligence in business will be a part of his religion, and he will enjoy the fulfilment of the promise, " the hand of the diligent maketh rich." True, his religion will keep him from all double dealing and dishonesty, and so he may not rise as rapidly as the wicked sometimes do, but then neither will he fall so ignominiously as they.

Believe not, therefore, my young friends, that your allegiance to God will interfere with true, abiding, commercial success. Even if it were to do so, it would still be your duty to be true to God. But it will not. God's providence is moral, and if you make a fair induction of facts you will find that, other things being equal, the religious man is all in all, and, in the long-run, the most prosperous as well as the happiest of merchants. I know that this is a low view of the matter, but I know, also, that the insinuations to which I have referred are made by those who would seduce you from the paths of integrity, and therefore I have taken the trouble to refute their reasoning. Do not allow yourselves to be led away by their plausibilities. Probe them to the bottom and you will see their falsity ; and remain true to Him who has said not only, " Blessed are the pure in heart for they shall see God," but also, " Blessed are the meek for they shall inherit the earth."

And now I conclude. When I began this book I was afraid to touch that exquisite story which was the favourite of our childhood, lest I should dim its beauty or destroy its charm. But it has become only the more interesting as we have examined it the more minutely; and the lessons which we have found in it have been so important that I am not without the hope that many will be permanently benefited by their consideration. In such a case the profit is yours, the joy is mine, and the praise is God's. Two things I trust we have learned. These are, to value above all others this ancient book, which, given by inspiration of God, has been found to be " profitable for doctrine, for reproof, for correction, for instruction in righteousness," and to resolve that we will suffer no criticism to nibble away from us the precious histories which are therein recorded.

INDEX.

AFFLICTION disposes to sympathy, 75.

Anderson, Lieutenant, quoted, 27.

Andrews, Bishop, quoted, 178.

Asher, blessing of, 185.

Auberlen, C. A., quoted, 226.

BAKER, chief, 64; dream of, 69; execution of, 71.

Baker, Sir Samuel, quoted, 36.

Beginning of sin, 31.

Beheading, death by, 71.

Beneficiaries, short memories of, 77.

Beni Hassan, representation on one of the tombs at, 14.

Benjamin not sent with his brothers to Egypt at first, 112; presence of, insisted on by Joseph, 116; received by Joseph, 129; Joseph's cup found in sack of, 132; intercession of Judah for, 132, 138; blessing of, by Jacob, 188.

Binney, Rev. Thomas, quoted, 91, 92, 97.

Birthday celebrations among the Egyptians, 72.

Browne, Bishop, quoted, 185.

Bruce, Michael, quoted, 172.

Brugsch, quoted or referred to, 40, 42, 88, 101.

Burial, Egyptian manner of, 198.

Bushnell, Horace, D.D., quoted, 72.

Business, important, should be done at once, 170.

Butler, chief, dream of, 63; dream of, and its fulfilment, 69; forgets Joseph, 71; speaks of Joseph to Pharaoh, 85.

CALLING, an honest, not a thing to be ashamed of, 153.

Campbell, Thomas, quoted, 174.

Captain of the guard, 45, 63.

Captivities, various kinds of, 47; what to do in, 49.

Chabas, M., quoted, 39, 42, 164.

Charon, origin of fable of, 198.

Character the true success in life, 62; relation of, to God's providence 73, 74; often tested when we do not know it, 135.

Cisterns in Palestine, 27.

Commentary, Bishop Ellicott's, quoted, 158.

—— Pulpit, 128; Jamieson, Fausset, and Browne, quoted, 90, 200.

" Commentary, Speakers'," quoted, 88, 90, 92, 105, 181, 182.

Contemporary Review, quoted, 39-42, 164.

Cooke, Canon, quoted, 88.

Corn policy of Joseph, 101-106.

DAN, blessing of, by Jacob, 184.

Diodorus referred to, 101, 198.

Devotion of Joseph to his father, 217.

Dods, Marcus, D.D., quoted, 60, 68, 141.

Donellan Lectures, by William Lee, D.D., quoted, 158, 159.

Dothan, 24.

Dreams, 65.

EBERS, referred to, 69.

Egypt, extent of, 35 ; name of, 35 ; inhabitants of, 38 ; early history of, 38 ; manners and customs of, 51, 62, 83, 89, 128, 147.

Egyptian waggons, 144.

Egyptian words in Genesis, 88.

Envy, course of, 22 ; nature of, 31.

Ephraim, birth of, 95 ; blessed by Jacob, 165.

Eternity of God a comfort in bereavement, 220-224

FABER, F. W., quoted, 62.

Fairbairn's " Imperial Bible Dictionary " quoted, 46, 157.

Faith, importance of, in death, 172.

Famines in Egypt, 99-101 ; causes of, 111.

Father and son, intercourse between, 227.

Favouritism, evil of, in the family, 16.

Forgiveness, difficulty of, 210.

Forgiving spirit of Joseph, 233.

GAD, blessing of, 185.

Gathered to his fathers, meaning of, 193.

Geikie, Cunningham, D.D., quoted, 69, 70, 71.

Genesis, different sections in the book of, 11 ; Egyptian words in, 88.

Goshen, Land of, 148.

Grave, locality of the, unimportant, 162.

Greeley, Horace, advice of, 152.

HANNA, DR. WILLIAM, quoted, 10.

Henry, Matthew, quoted, 58.

Herodotus referred to, 102.

" Herodotus," Rawlinson's, quoted, 200.

Hyksos, or Shepherd kings of Egypt, 39.

INTERCESSION of Judah for Benjamin, 132, 139.

Intercourse between a father and a grown-up son, 161, 170.

Interpretation of the dream of the chief butler and chief baker, 70 ; of the dreams of Pharaoh, 86.

Inundation of the Nile, 36.

Isaac some years contemporary with Joseph, 11 ; probable effect of intercourse with, on Joseph, 12 ; encampment of, at Hebron, 12.

Issachar, blessing of, 183, 191.

JACOB, effect of Peniel upon, 9 ; goes to Shechem, 10 ; encampment of, at Hebron, 13 ; gives a peculiar dress to Joseph, 14 ; sends Joseph to seek his brothers, 23 ; sends his ten sons to Egypt for food, 112 ; laments over the absence of Simeon, 119 ; sends his sons a second time to Egypt, 126 ; removal of, with his family, to Egypt, 145 ; halt of, at Beersheba, 146 ; met by Joseph, 146 ; interview of, with Pharaoh, 148, 150 ; visited by Joseph alone, 161 ; requests to be buried in Machpelah, 162 ; reasons of, for this request, 163 ; takes an oath of Joseph, 163 ; blesses Ephraim and Manasseh, 165 ; faith of, 167, 172 ; blesses his sons, 174-192 ; death of, 193 ; embalmment of the body of, 199 ; burial of, 204 ; character of, 204 ; contrasted with that of King Saul, 206.

Joseph contemporary with Isaac for some years, 12 ; receives a peculiar coat from Jacob, 14 ; brings to his father the evil report of his brothers, 14 ; dreams of, 15 ; antagonism of his brothers to, 17 ; sent to seek his brothers, 23; reception of, by his brothers, 25; put into a pit, 27; sold to the Ishmaelites, 28; first position of, in Egypt, 44; purchased by Potiphar, 45; time of service with Potiphar, 50; temptation of, 51-53; triumph of, 53; in the prison, 54; interprets the dreams of the chief butler and the chief baker, 70; waiting in the prison, 78-81; sent for by Pharaoh, 80; in the presence of the king, 86; interprets Pharaoh's dreams, 86; promoted to the second place in the kingdom, 87; receives a new name, 88; feelings of, at the birth of his children, 94, 95; forgetfulness of his father by, 96; corn policy of, 101-106; reception of his brothers by, 113; conceals his relationship from his brothers, 114-117; keeps Simeon as a hostage, 118; receives his brothers on their second visit, 128; explanation of his conduct to his brothers, 114, 130; divining cup of, 131; tender regard of, for Jacob, 142; makes himself known to his brothers, 143; sends his brothers back to Canaan, 143; receives his father in Egypt, 117; visits his father alone, 161; visits his father with his two sons, 135; receives a special portion from his father, 168; blessing of, by Jacob, 186; buries his father at Machpelah, 204; returns to Egypt, 209; character of, not understood by his brothers, 211; equanimity of, 216; gives commandment concerning his remains, 218; character and career of, 225; devotion of, to his father, 226; recognition of the constant presence of God by, 228; moral courage of, 230; patience of, 231; forgiving spirit of, 233; piety of, 234; success of, 236.

KALISCH quoted, 128.
Kitto, Dr. John, quoted, 45, 54, 111.

LAKE, sacred, 198.
Lange's Genesis quoted, 31.
Lawson, George, D.D., quoted, 21.
Lee, Dr. W., Donellan Lectures quoted, 159, 160.
Lepsius referred to, 42.
Levi, blessing of, 178.
Lewis, Taylor, quoted, 32.
Life, brevity of, 154.
Life, outer, different from inner, 137.

MANASSEH, birth of, 11; blessed by Jacob, 167.
Machpelah, Cave of, request of Jacob to be buried in, 162; description of mosque above, 201; burial of Jacob in, 201.
Moral courage of Joseph, 230.
Mourning, Egyptian, 200.

NÂBLUS, 22, 168.
Naphtali, blessing of, 186.
Nile, sources of the, 36; inundation of the, explained, 37; importance of the, to Egypt, 38, 84.
Nile, the Black, 36; the Blue, 36; the White, 36.

PATIENCE of Joseph, 231.
Peniel, effect of night at, upon Jacob, 7.
Pharaoh sends for Joseph, 83; dream of, 84; exalts Joseph to the second place, 87; receives Jacob, 148.
Piety of Joseph not incompatible with strength and manliness, 234.
Plan of God in every man's life, 71, 72.
Poole, R. S., quoted, 39-42.

Potiphar purchases Joseph, 45 ; captain of the guard, 45.

Potiphar's wife the temptress of Joseph, 51 ; falsely accuses Joseph, 51.

Prayer a support in trial, 124.

Providence, minute particularity of, 71, 213 ; relation of character to, 73, 74, 189 ; works through men's sins, 81, 214 ; and through trial, 122 ; is not to be judged of before the time, 123.

Public administration of Joseph, 91-106.

Purposes of God helped towards fulfilment by men's efforts to defeat them, 32.

RACHEL, reference of Jacob to, on his death-bed, 166.

Recognition of God's presence by Joseph, 228.

Residence, change of, to be made with the sanction of God, 151.

Responsibility for what we see and hear in others, 19 ; not got rid of by putting the trust out of sight, 33.

Reuben, effort of, to save Joseph, 25 ; grief of, at the failure of his plan, 29, 118 ; offer of, to bring Benjamin back, 127 ; blessing of, 177.

Right to be done irrespective of consequences, 62.

Robinson, Rev. Dr. Edward, quoted, 103.

SCOTT, SIR WALTER, quoted, 61.

Shakespeare quoted, 22, 67, 114.

Shechem described, 10, 22.

Shepherds, Egyptian, prejudice against, 147.

Shiloh, meaning of, 180.

Simeon retained by Joseph, 117 ; restored, 129 ; blessing of, 178, 189.

Sin, beginning of, 31.

Slave market, Joseph in the, 44.

Smith's " Dictionary of the Bible " quoted, 24, 43, 100.

Smith, Rev. Thornley, 101, 111, 145, 197.

" Speakers' Commentary," quoted, 88, 90, 102. 105, 181, 182.

Staff, bowing on the, meaning of, 40, 164, 165.

Stanley, Dean, 202.

Success in life, true, 62, 92 ; way to, not closed against any man, 90.

TABLE, genealogical, in Genesis xlvi. 10-29, 156.

Taylor, Isaac, quoted, 114.

Temptation, how to meet, 56.

Temptation of Joseph, 51-53 ; general lessons from the, 55-62.

Tennyson quoted, 194, 195.

Thomson, W. H., M.D., LL.D., quoted, 181, 188.

Thomson, W. M., D.D., quoted, 23, 24, 27.

Tower of London, illustration from, 77.

Trench, Archbishop, quoted, 207, 208.

UNCERTAINTIES of human existence, 30.

WAGGONS, Egyptian, 145.

Wilberforce, Bishop, quoted, 206.

Wilkinson, Sir J. G., quoted, 51, 69, 83, 89, 128, 147, 196, 197, 199.

Will, importance of making a, 171.

Words, Egyptian, in Genesis, 88.

ZAPHNATH-PAANEAH, meaning of, 88.

Zebulon, blessing of, 182.